THE
STORY OF LIBERTY

AMERICA'S HERITAGE THROUGH THE CIVIL WAR

BY JOHN DE GREE

STUDENT EDITION

PART 2

Table of Contents

FOREWORD

Young American history students and their teachers have long yearned for a book like the one you now hold in your hands. John De Gree's The Story of Liberty, From America's Heritage through the Civil War, is a well-researched, ably-written, and sensible depiction of American history from the founding through the Civil War. What do I mean by "sensible"? Simply this: John relates the truth about the American past by telling about our many good qualities and accomplishments as well as the setbacks our nation has endured during its long history. Few books as good as this one have been published for young readers. At last we have a new, up-to-date book suitable for American middle school and high school history students.

When Larry Schweikart and I first published our #1 New York Times best-selling book, A Patriot's History of the United States, we succeeded in filling a similar void existing in college-level American history books. Larry and I have often said that American history is not the story of, to use an old folk saying, a "half-empty cup." Indeed, we argued that the American cup was nearly full. Americans have made great mistakes, but they have also done much that is good. American patriots in 1776 created a democratic republic governed by ordinary citizens at a time in history when absolutist monarchs ruled most of Europe, all-powerful Czars, Emperors, and Shoguns tyrannized Russia and the Far East, and some Middle Eastern and North African monarchs claimed divine authority and direct links to God. While it is true that Americans allowed the enslavement of African-American people, they ultimately fought a bloody war that ended slavery forever. While American soldiers killed native Indians and pushed them westward onto reservations, American diplomats signed legally binding treaties that those Indians' descendants use to their great benefit in courts today. And while there has been poverty and suffering in our country's history, it pales in comparison to that of the rest of the world. It is no accident that, for over 400 years, millions of foreigners have yearned and sought to become Americans.

John De Gree tells about this and much more in The Story of Liberty, From America's Heritage through the Civil War. He traces our nation's past from the time of the Pilgrims through the Colonial era and the American Revolution. He explains Jeffersonian and Jacksonian politics and the critical events leading to the Civil War. And he narrates the military and political history of that pivotal conflict. De Gree has a unique way of telling the story of the United States. He places special emphasis on America's place in the history of advancing Western Civilization. He begins with our classical roots and ties to ancient Hebrew, Greek, Roman, and Western European institutions. Just as importantly, he accurately weaves the story of Christianity and Christian values into the American story. No truthful history of the United States of America can ignore this vital religious element.

I first met John De Gree nearly a decade ago when we collaborated on curriculum for the growing number of homeschool, charter, private, and public school students who utilize his Classical Historian method. I remain impressed with his intellect and work ethic, and the range of exciting, effective tools he offers modern students of American history and their teachers. I am confident The Story of Liberty, From America's Heritage through the Civil War, will become a very successful textbook in educating a future generation of American patriots.

Michael Allen, Ph.D.
University of Washington, Tacoma, 2017

NORTH AMERICA, 1783

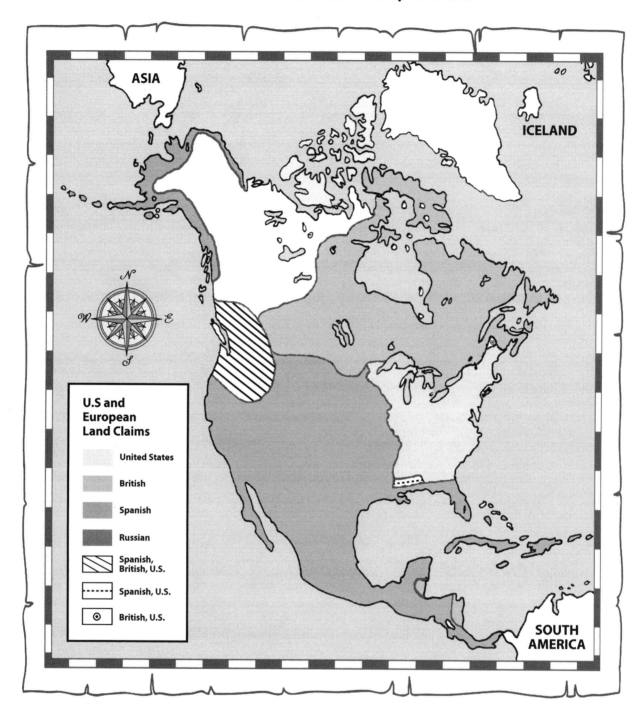

ASIA

ICELAND

U.S and European Land Claims

- United States
- British
- Spanish
- Russian
- Spanish, British, U.S.
- Spanish, U.S.
- British, U.S.

SOUTH AMERICA

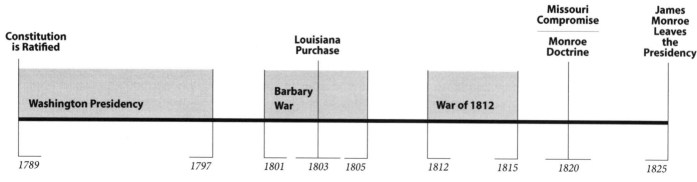

Constitution is Ratified

Louisiana Purchase

Missouri Compromise

Monroe Doctrine

James Monroe Leaves the Presidency

Washington Presidency

Barbary War

War of 1812

1789   1797   1801   1803   1805   1812   1815   1820   1825

CHAPTER 31

Ratification of the Constitution

The Signing of the Constitution

James Madison

Grammar
What You Need to Know

1. **Federalists:** The Federalists wanted a strong, federal government and favored the Constitution. John Jay, Alexander Hamilton, and James Madison were Federalists.

2. **Anti-Federalists:** The Anti-Federalists were against the Constitution and wanted a weaker federal government and stronger state governments. Patrick Henry, Thomas Jefferson, Sam Adams, and James Monroe were Anti-Federalists.

3. **Bill of Rights:** The Bill of Rights is a list of 10 individual and states' rights the federal government can never infringe upon. They are the first ten amendments to the Constitution.

4. ***The Federalist Papers:*** John Jay, Alexander Hamilton, and James Madison wrote a series of essays to persuade Americans to adopt the Constitution.

5. **Faction:** A faction is a group of people united by a single cause and they try to influence the government to agree with their cause. A faction is an interest group.

6. **Despotism:** Despotism is another way of saying tyranny. Despotism is when the government totally controls its citizens and there is no freedom.

7. **Term limits:** A term limit is a limit of how many times a politician can be elected to one office. The President has a term limit of two terms.

8. **Father of the Constitution:** James Madison is the principal author of the Constitution.

LOGIC
READING COMPREHENSION AND INFERENCE QUESTIONS

1. According to the Articles of Confederation,

      a. The ratification of the Constitution went against the law.

      b. 9 out of 13 states had to approve the Constitution so it would be ratified.

      c. The states could legally never ratify the Constitution.

      d. A President could only serve two terms.

Answer:

Which sentence(s) best supports your answer?

_____

_____

_____

2. According to the authors of *The Federalist Papers*,

      a. The Articles of Confederation lacked a weak President.

      b. The Articles of Confederation lacked a strong President.

      c. The Articles of Confederation lacked a President.

      d. The Articles of Confederation lacked a war.

Answer:

Which sentence(s) best supports your answer?

_____

_____

3. According to the authors of *The Federalist Papers*,

      a. The states would become unimportant.

      b. The states would relinquish most power to the federal government.

      c. The states would encourage military service.

      d. Americans' religious nature would ensure no tyrant could ever take over.

Answer:

Which sentence(s) best supports your answer?

_____

_____

4. According to the Anti-Federalists, in the new Constitution,

a. the President shouldn't have any term limits.

b. the Judiciary Branch wasn't strong enough.

c. The states' role was unfortunately diminished.

d. The central government wasn't strong enough.

Answer:

Which sentence(s) best supports your answer?

_____

_____

5. According to the lesson, you can infer the author thinks

a. the Constitution created a federal government that is too strong.

b. the Constitution created a federal government that is too weak.

c. the arguments between the Federalists and Anti-Federalists continue.

d. the Anti-Federalist had more Founding Fathers than the Federalists.

Answer: **c**

Which sentence(s) best supports your answer?

_____

_____

_____

RHETORIC
SHORT ANSWER QUESTIONS

Answer the following with a short essay (3-5 sentences):

1. How did the education of the Founding Fathers influence the creation of the Constitution?

_____

_____

_____

_____

_____

2. What argument of the Anti-Federalists do you find as most persuasive? Why?

Answer:

_____

_____

_____

_____

_____

3. Did the Anti-Federalists completely fail in their debate with the Federalists over the ratification of the Constitution?

Answer:

_____

_____

_____

_____

_____

_____

_____

NORTH AMERICA, 1783

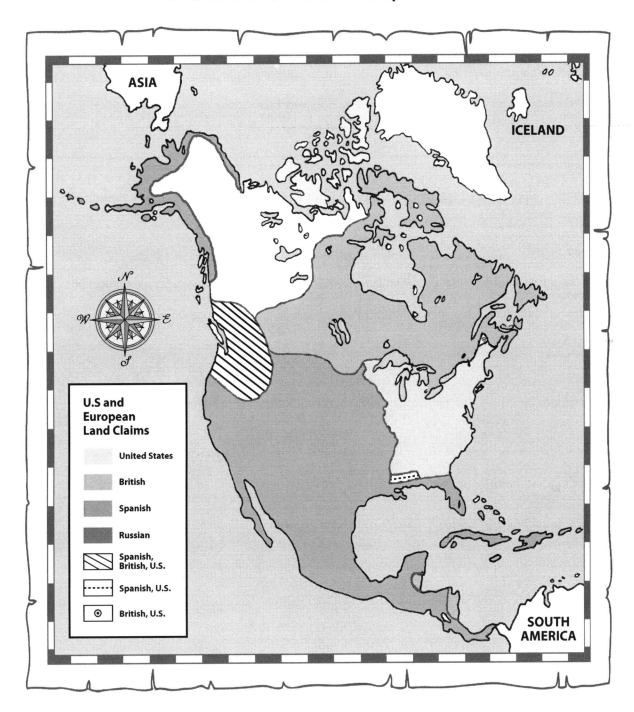

U.S and
European
Land Claims

- United States
- British
- Spanish
- Russian
- Spanish, British, U.S.
- Spanish, U.S.
- British, U.S.

Answer these questions and test your map knowledge.

1. In 1789, which country controlled the most land in North America? _____

2. In 1789, which countries bordered the U.S.A? _____

3. Which Asian country controled part of North America in 1789? _____

4. Which country bordered the north of the U.S.A? _____

5. Which country bordered the east and south of the U.S.A? _____

THE AMERICAN PEOPLE, 1800

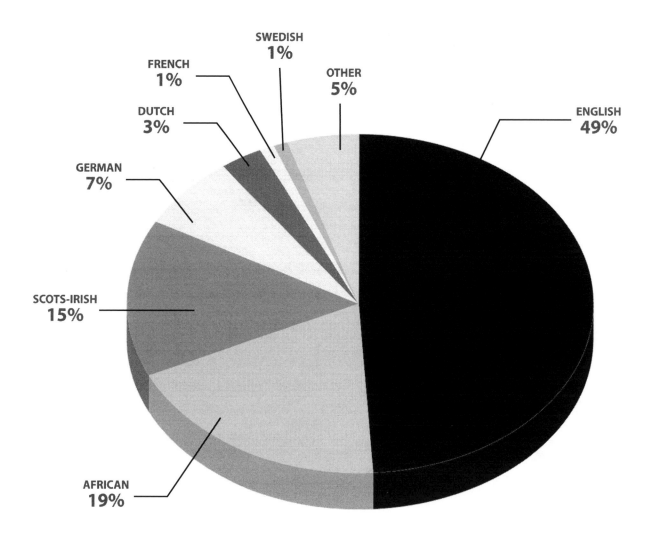

SWEDISH
1%

FRENCH
1%

OTHER
5%

DUTCH
3%

ENGLISH
49%

GERMAN
7%

SCOTS-IRISH
15%

AFRICAN
19%

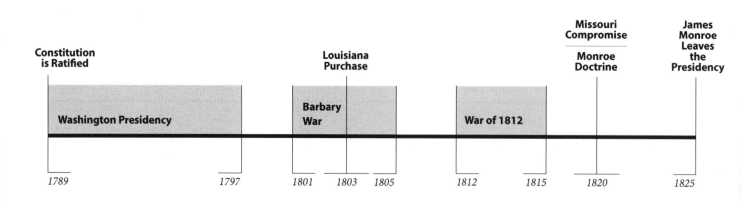

Constitution
is Ratified

Louisiana
Purchase

Missouri
Compromise

James
Monroe
Leaves
the
Presidency

Monroe
Doctrine

Washington Presidency

Barbary
War

War of 1812

1789   1797   1801   1803   1805   1812   1815   1820   1825

CHAPTER 32

THE AMERICAN PEOPLE

Frontiersman

Farmhouse

GRAMMAR
WHAT YOU NEED TO KNOW

1. 1790 population: 4,000,000

2. 1890 population: 70,000,000

3. Conestoga Wagon: Many Americans moved west in a Conestoga Wagon.

4. Slave Population: In the early 1800s, 1/7 of Americans were slaves.

5. Republican Party: This party wanted a limited, federal government and was led by Thomas Jefferson, James Monroe, and James Madison.

6. Federalist Party: This party wanted a strong, federal government and was led by Alexander Hamilton, John Adams, and John Marshall.

7. Sailboat: Travel by sailboat was the fastest means of travel in the early 1800s.

1. Based on the lesson, what is one reason Americans did not have an extensive police force in the early 1800s?

      a. Most Americans were Buddhists who believed in the same ideas of morality.

      b. Most Americans were Jews who believed in the same ideas of morality.

      c. Most Americans were atheists who had different ideas of morality.

      d. Most Americans were of the same religion and had very similar ideas of morality.

Answer:

Which sentence(s) best supports this answer:

_____

_____

_____

2. Based on the lesson, you can infer that in the early 1800s most Americans

      a. received a paycheck.

      b. worked for someone else.

      c. had business skills.

      d. couldn't read that well.

Answer:

Which sentence(s) best supports this answer:

_____

_____

_____

3. In the early 1800s, if an American needed to travel west, most likely, how would he travel?

      a. by boat

      b. by sailboat

      c. by wagon

      d. by train

Answer:

Which sentence(s) best supports this answer:

_____

_____

RHETORIC
SHORT ANSWER QUESTIONS

Answer the following with a short essay (3-5 sentences):

1. In the early 1800s, how much was the federal government involved in the lives of Americans?

_____

_____

_____

_____

_____

2. Based on the lesson, how would you describe most Americans, in terms of religion?

_____

_____

_____

_____

_____

_____

_____

3. Was slavery common and widespread in America in the early 1800s?

_____

_____

THE AMERICAN PEOPLE, 1800

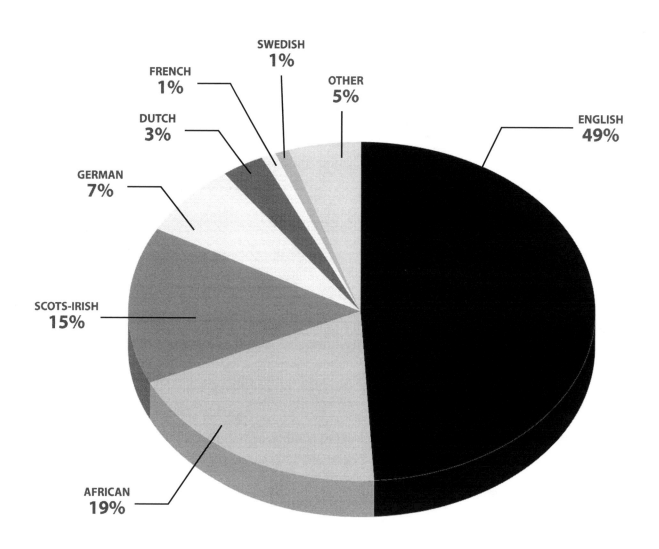

Answer these questions and test your knowledge.

1. What percentage of the American people in 1800 were English? 49%

What percentage of the American people in 1800 were African? 19%

3. What percentage of the American people in 1800 were French? 1%

4. What percentage of the American people in 1800 were Scots-Irish? 15%

5. What percentage of the American people in 1800 were Dutch? 3%

NOTES

THE UNITED STATES OF AMERICA, 1790

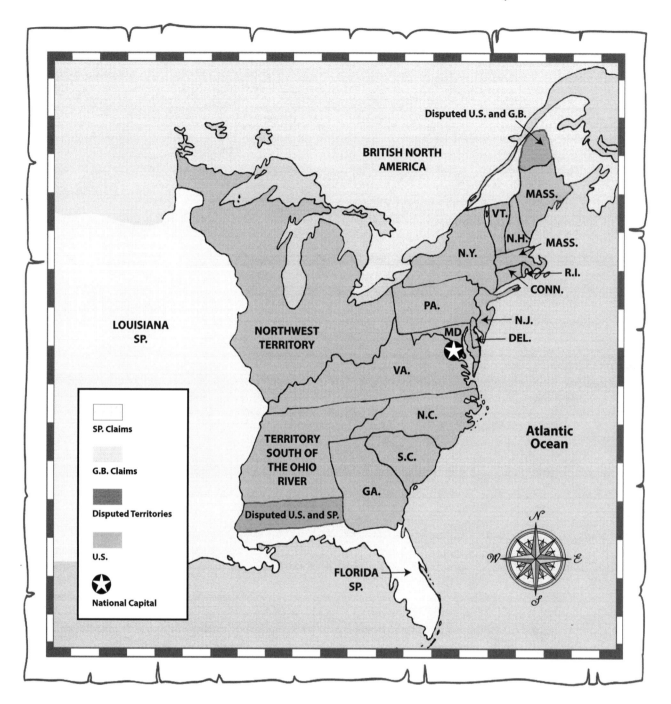

Disputed U.S. and G.B.

BRITISH NORTH AMERICA

MASS.

VT.

N.H.

MASS.

N.Y.

R.I.

CONN.

PA.

N.J.

MD

DEL.

LOUISIANA SP.

NORTHWEST TERRITORY

VA.

N.C.

Atlantic Ocean

TERRITORY SOUTH OF THE OHIO RIVER

S.C.

GA.

Disputed U.S. and SP.

FLORIDA SP.

SP. Claims

G.B. Claims

Disputed Territories

U.S.

National Capital

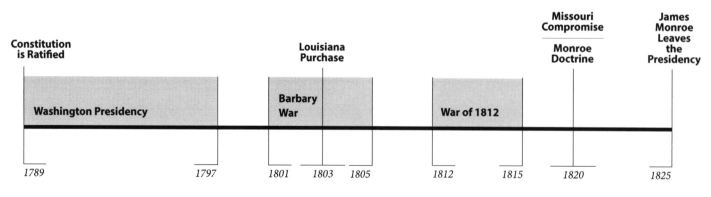

Constitution is Ratified

Louisiana Purchase

Missouri Compromise

Monroe Doctrine

James Monroe Leaves the Presidency

Washington Presidency

Barbary War

War of 1812

1789   1797   1801   1803   1805   1812   1815   1820   1825

CHAPTER 33

FATHER OF THE COUNTRY

George Washington

GRAMMAR
WHAT YOU NEED TO KNOW

1. Washington Presidency: 1789-1787.

2. Cabinet: The Cabinet is a group of advisors to the President. Washington started this tradition.

3. Alexander Hamilton: Hamilton was the first Secretary of the Treasury and promoted a strong, federal government.

4. Thomas Jefferson: Jefferson was the first Secretary of State and wanted strong state governments.

5. Whiskey Rebellion: In the Whiskey Rebellion, Pennsylvania farmers revolted against a federal tax and Washington suppressed the rebellion with 13,000 soldiers.

6. French Revolution: In 1789, the French removed the French King, beheaded him, and embarked on a bloody and radical revolution that ended with the Napoleonic Wars.

7. Washington's Farewell Address: Washington warned against political parties and against fighting in foreign wars before the American military is ready.

8. Republicans: Republicans tended to be farmers, wanted a weaker navy and army, and tended to be pro-slavery.

9. Federalists: Federalists wanted a stronger, central government, tended to be anti-slavery, and were mainly merchants and bankers.

10. Debt: Debt is the amount of money government or people owe.

1. According to the lesson, what can you infer was the main reason the American Revolution didn't follow the bloody pattern of typical revolutions?

        a. The British behaved themselves.

        b. Thomas Jefferson

        c. The Americans behaved themselves.

        d. George Washington

Answer:

Which sentence(s) best supports this answer?

_____

_____

_____

2. Based on the lesson, the author thinks political parties

        a. are terrible.

        b. are wonderful.

        c. are not natural.

        d. are ordinary.

Answer:

Which sentence(s) best supports this answer?

_____

_____

_____

3. If you were an American in 1792 and wanted the U.S. government to assume all state debt from the war, you would most likely be a

        a. Farmer

        b. Merchant

        c. Southerner

        d. Slave owner

Answer:

Where did you find your answer?

_____

_____

4. Based on the lesson, you can infer the banking policies of Alexander Hamilton were

      a. a main reason for the success of the young United States of America.

      b. a main reason for the failure of the young United States of America.

      c. confusing.

      d. loved by Thomas Jefferson and the Republicans.

Answer:

Which sentence(s) best supports this answer:

_____

_____

_____

5. Based on Washington's Farewell Address, Washington

      a. wanted America to never get in a war.

      b. wanted America to immediately get involved in a war, if it was just.

      c. wanted America to get strong before it engaged another country in war.

      d. wanted America to stay in isolation from the world's problems.

Answer: **c**

Which sentence(s) best supports this answer?

_____

_____

_____

RHETORIC
SHORT ANSWER QUESTIONS

Answer the following with a short essay (3-5 sentences):

1. Why did Washington choose men who might have been smarter than he was to be in his Cabinet?

Answer:

_____

_____

2. How did selling bonds to Americans encourage the wealthy to care about the success of the United States of America?

Answer:

_____

_____

_____

_____

_____

3. Did George Washington warn Americans against all war in his Farewell Address?

Answer:

_____

_____

_____

_____

_____

_____

_____

_____

MAP WORK
TEST YOUR KNOWLEDGE

Practice drawing and labeling the map, until you can do so by memory.

THE UNITED STATES OF AMERICA, 1790

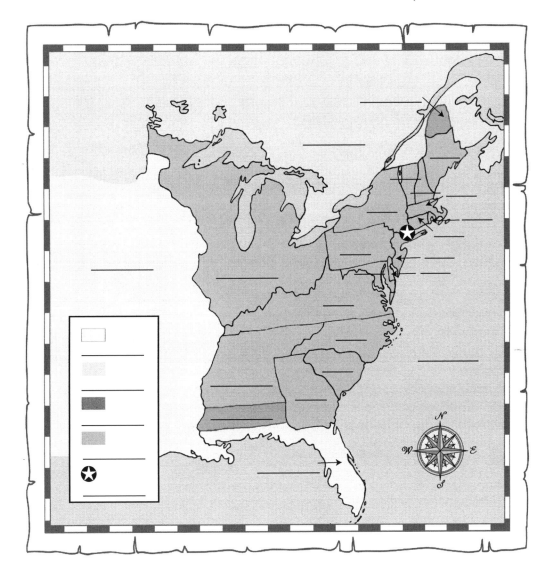

Answer these questions and test your map knowledge.

1. In 1790, which country controlled Louisiana? _____

2. In 1790, which country controlled Florida? _____

3. In 1790, which country controlled the Northwest Territory? _____

4. According to the map, which state appears the largest in terms of land area? _____

5. Which two states border Washington, D.C? _____

XYZ Affair

During John Adams' Presidency,
France seized American ships carrying goods to British ports.
Napoleon Bonaparte of France wanted to take over Great Britain.

To avert war, Adams sent a peace commission to Paris.

French foreign minister Talleyrand demanded the Americans
pay his three French agents $250,000 and promise to loan France
$12 million just to talk to the French. Americans learned of this
and called the French agents "X, Y, and Z."

Americans were outraged at this bribe request and
responded with the sentiment, "Millions for defense,
not one cent for tribute."

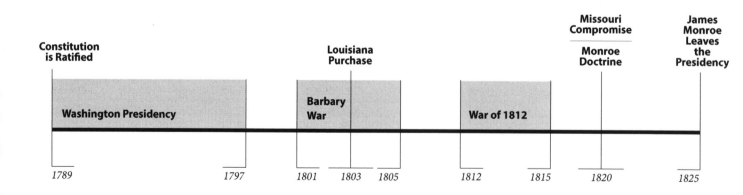

Constitution is Ratified — Washington Presidency — Louisiana Purchase — Barbary War — War of 1812 — Missouri Compromise — Monroe Doctrine — James Monroe Leaves the Presidency

1789 — 1797 — 1801 — 1803 — 1805 — 1812 — 1815 — 1820 — 1825

CHAPTER 34

PRESIDENCY OF JOHN ADAMS, 1797-1801

John Adams

GRAMMAR
WHAT YOU NEED TO KNOW

1. **Quasi War:** Great Britain and France waged naval war against the USA and the USA didn't respond. Quasi means "apparently but not really."

2. **Alien and Sedition Acts:** The Alien and Sedition Acts were a number of laws that limited the free speech of journalists and all Americans and made it harder to immigrate to the USA.

3. **Election of 1800:** Republican Thomas Jefferson beat Federalist John Adams, and it was the first time that presidential power changed political parties peacefully in the world in over 1700 years.

4. **John Adams' Presidency:** John Adams was President from 1797-1801.

1. According to the lesson, who or what was most responsible for the peaceful passage of power in 1797?

      a. John Adams

      b. Thomas Jefferson

      c. George Washington

      d. Patrick Henry

Answer:

Which sentence(s) best supports this answer?

_____

_____

_____

2. Based on the lesson, you can infer that America did not start a war against France and Britain because

      a. Americans did not like violence.

      b. Americans did not want to get involved in a foreign war.

      c. Americans were afraid of Indians.

      d. America would have probably lost the war.

Answer:

Which sentence(s) best supports this answer?

_____

_____

3. Based on your knowledge of the Constitution gained in an earlier chapter, which amendment did the Alien and Sedition Acts go against?

      a. First Amendment

      b. Second Amendment

      c. Third Amendment

      d. Fourth Amendment

Answer:

Which sentence(s) best supports your answer?

_____

_____

4. Based on the lesson, which exchange of power was more important?

      a. From Washington's Presidency to Adams'

      b. From Adams' Presidency to Jefferson's

Answer:

Which sentence(s) best supports your answer?

_____

_____

_____

5. Place the events in chronological order:

      a. Quasi War

      b. Washington chosen President

      c. Jefferson chosen President

      d. Adams chosen President

Answer:

RHETORIC
SHORT ANSWER QUESTIONS

Answer the following with a short essay (3-5 sentences):

1. What made the exchanges of power in 1797 and 1801 unique?

Answer:

_____

_____

_____

_____

_____

_____

2. Was John Adams a weak President, because of his unwillingness to engage America in war against the French and British?

Answer:

_____

_____

_____

_____

_____

3. How were the Alien and Sedition Acts a violation of the First Amendment?

Answer:

_____

_____

_____

_____

_____

XYZ Affair

During John Adams' Presidency,
France seized American ships carrying goods to British ports.
Napoleon Bonaparte of France wanted to take over Great Britain.

To avert war, Adams sent a peace commission to Paris.

French foreign minister Talleyrand demanded the Americans
pay his three French agents $250,000 and promise to loan France
$12 million just to talk to the French. Americans learned of this
and called the French agents "X, Y, and Z."

Americans were outraged at this bribe request and
responded with the sentiment, "Millions for defense,
not one cent for tribute."

Answer these questions and test your knowledge.

1. Who wanted to take over Great Britain? _____

2. To which country did Adams send a peace commission? _____

3. Who was France's foreign minister at the time? _____

4. What did Talleyrand demand in order for the Americans to speak with the French?

_____

5. What was the American sentiment towards Talleyrand's demand? _____

_____

U.S. Population by Region, 1790 - 1900

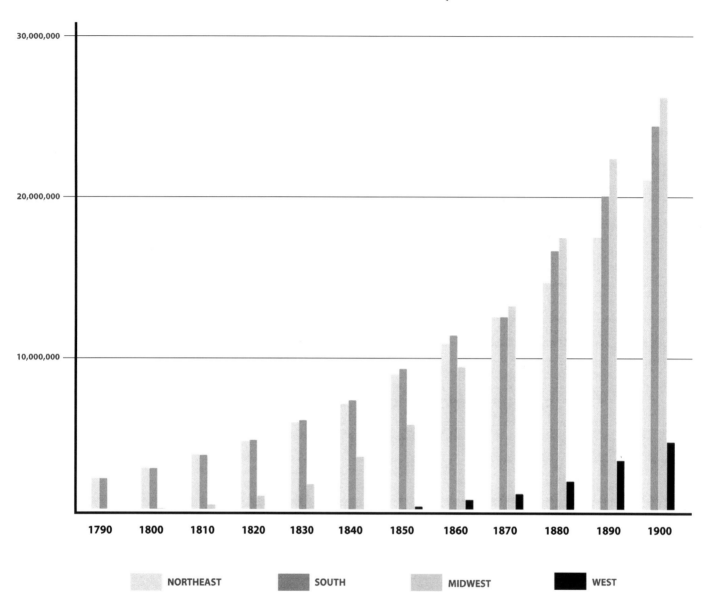

NORTHEAST **SOUTH** **MIDWEST** **WEST**

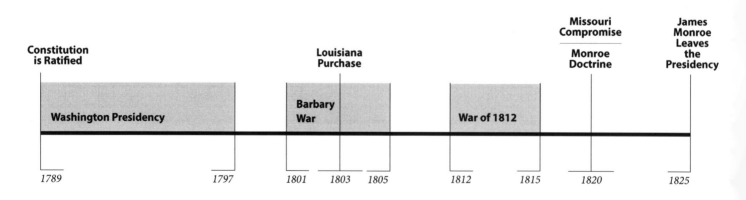

Constitution is Ratified

Louisiana Purchase

Missouri Compromise

Monroe Doctrine

James Monroe Leaves the Presidency

Washington Presidency

Barbary War

War of 1812

1789 *1797* *1801* *1803* *1805* *1812* *1815* *1820* *1825*

CHAPTER 35

THE SUPREME COURT, JUDICIAL REVIEW, AND CAPITALISM

Supreme Court

GRAMMAR
WHAT YOU NEED TO KNOW

1. **Judicial Review:** This is the power the Supreme Court has to interpret a law and decide if it is constitutional or unconstitutional. Judicial review is not found in the Constitution.

2. **Marbury v. Madison, 1803:** In this Supreme Court decision, the Supreme Court gave itself the power of judicial review.

3. **Dartmouth College v. Woodward, 1819:** This Supreme Court decision established that a contract cannot be voided, and it helped establish capitalism, free enterprise, and open markets in America.

4. **Capitalism:** Capitalism is a set of principles and behavior of people based on the principles of individual and property rights.

5. **Free Market:** The free market is a place where individuals can buy and sell items or services, as each person thinks is best. It is an economy where each person chooses what to do with his money, time, and talent.

6. **Intentions of the Founding Fathers regarding economy:** The Founding Fathers wanted to create a society where individuals could pursue their interests and passions, and where a strong government, like a King, could not dictate to others.

7. **Slavery and the Free Market:** Slavery is an institution that goes directly against the free market, because slaves have no freedom what to do with their time and talent, and any money.

LOGIC
READING COMPREHENSION AND INFERENCE QUESTIONS

1. Based on the lesson, you can infer that capitalism in America was

      a. better for the average man than the economic system in Great Britain.

      b. worse for the average man than the economic system in Great Britain.

      c. fair for the slaves.

      d. had nothing to do with slavery.

Answer:

Which sentence(s) best supports this answer?

_____

_____

2. Based on the lesson, you can infer that Chief Justice Marshall

      a. thought the Supreme Court should not get involved in important decisions.

      b. thought the Supreme Court should always favor the decisions of Jefferson.

      c. thought the Supreme Court should only follow what was written in the Constitution.

      d. thought the Supreme Court needed to be more powerful than what was written in the Constitution.

Answer:

Which sentence(s) best supports this answer?

_____

_____

3. Based on the lesson, you can infer Americans' knowledge of the Bible

      a. created a demented society.

      b. created a Biblical society.

      c. created a civil society without need of a large government.

      d. created a civil society with need of a large government.

Answer: **c**

Which sentence(s) best supports this answer?

_____

_____

_____

4. Based on the lesson, you can infer that in the early 1800s, children above the age of five or so

      a. were able to play all day.

      b. were not allowed to venture out of the sight of their mothers.

      c. had to be industrious.

      d. were lazy.

Answer:

Which sentence(s) best supports this answer?

_____

_____

_____

5. Based on the lesson, if you were a schoolchild in the early 1800s, you might

      a. go to a medical school.

      b. go to a farm to school.

      c. live with your instructor.

      d. not ever learn how to read and write.

Answer:

Which sentence(s) best supports this answer?

_____

_____

RHETORIC
SHORT ANSWER QUESTIONS

Answer the following with a short essay (3-5 sentences):

1. Based on the lesson, why did America become such a rich nation in the 1800s?

Answer:

_____

_____

_____

_____

_____

2. In a capitalist society, does the government choose who the "winners" will be?

Answer:

_____

_____

_____

_____

_____

3. Why is it important that the Supreme Court, in a series of cases, protected the inviolability of a contract?

Answer:

_____

_____

_____

_____

_____

_____

U.S. POPULATION BY REGION, 1790 - 1900

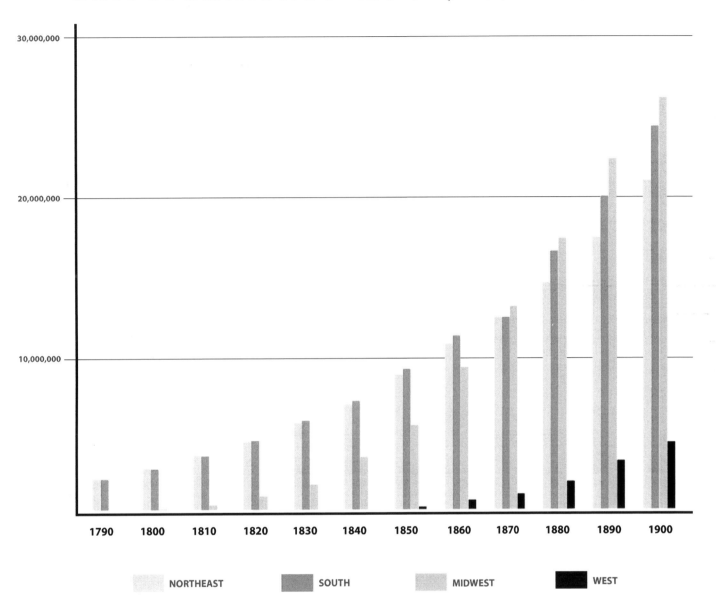

Answer these questions and test your knowledge.

1. In 1790, which two regions had the most people? _____

2. In 1900, which two regions had the most people? _____

3. From 1810 to 1860, which region grew the most? _____

4. In 1860, which region had the least amount of people? _____

5. When did the Midwest surpass the Northeast and South in population? _____

LOUISIANA PURCHASE, 1803

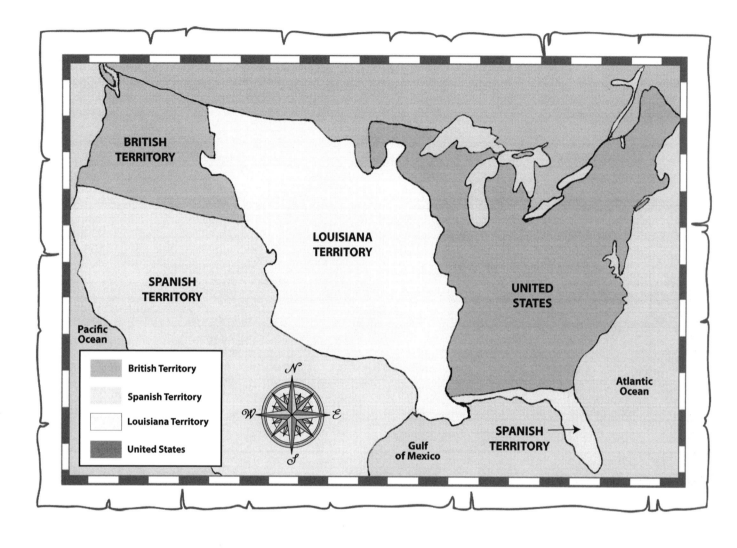

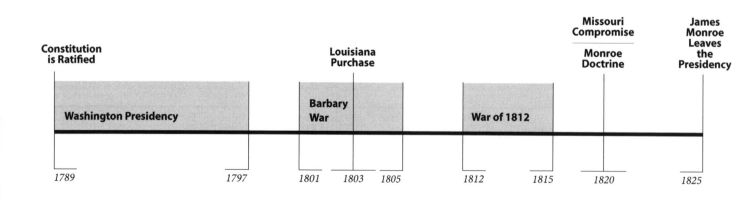

CHAPTER 36

PRESIDENCY OF THOMAS JEFFERSON (1801-1809)

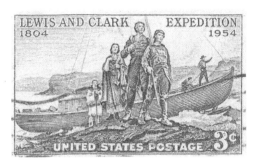

Lewis and Clark Expedition

Thomas Jefferson

WHAT YOU NEED TO KNOW

1. **Shaking hands:** Instead of bowing to others, as was the custom, Thomas Jefferson shook hands, to show that he was equal with others.

2. **The Great Migration:** The Great Migration was a mass movement of people to the west of the United States of America throughout the 1800s. The pace of migration sped up with Thomas Jefferson.

3. **Louisiana Purchase:** Thomas Jefferson purchased Louisiana from the French leader Napoleon, and it doubled the size of the U.S.A., in 1803.

4. **Lewis and Clark Expedition:** Jefferson commissioned Merriweather Lewis and William Clark to take military volunteers on an expedition through Louisiana to map new land, befriend Indian tribes and announce the arrival of the U.S.A., explore trade possibilities, and find and log new animal and plant species. The expedition lasted from 1804 to 1806.

5. **Sacagawea:** Sacagawea was the only female on the Lewis and Clark Expedition. She helped as a guide and was a sign to Indians that this was not a military expedition.

6. **Barbary War:** From 1801 to 1805, Jefferson led the U.S.A. in a war against the Barbary Pirates, attacking first and claiming victory against the Muslim pirates from Northern Africa.

7. **Embargo Act of 1807:** This act forbade Americans to trade with Great Britain or France and it greatly hurt American businesses.

LOGIC
READING COMPREHENSION AND INFERENCE QUESTIONS

1. Based on the lesson, you can infer the Barbary Pirates of the 1700s believed

    a. their Muslim religion did not allow them to have slaves.

    b. their religion justified their taking of slaves.

    c. Americans had many Muslim sailors.

    d. the American military was mighty.

Answer:

Which sentence(s) best supports this answer?

_____

_____

2. Based on the lesson, you can infer

    a. Jefferson believed America had to be attacked in order to start a war.

    b. Jefferson thought it could be just (good) to attack another country first.

    c. Jefferson was against war no matter the situation.

    d. Jefferson loved the military.

Answer:

Which sentence(s) best supports your answer?

_____

_____

3. Based on the lesson, you can infer

    a. The Lewis and Clark Expedition was a failure.

    b. It's expensive to try to conquer the world.

    c. Americans were greedy to buy all of Louisiana.

    d. Many Americans died moving west.

Answer:

Which sentence(s) best supports this answer?

_____

_____

4. Based on the lesson, you can infer that Jefferson

   a. was not a man to punish his political enemies.

   b. was a horrible President.

   c. loved to buy land.

   d. wanted to take away land from Indians.

Answer:

Which sentence(s) best supports the answer?

_____

_____

5. Which of the following did not entice immigrants to come to America in the 1800s?

   a. inexpensive land

   b. liberty

   c. free health care

   d. free markets

Answer:

Which sentence(s) best supports your answer?

_____

_____

RHETORIC
SHORT ANSWER QUESTIONS

Answer the following with a short essay (3-5 sentences):

1. Compare and contrast how Jefferson dealt with the Barbary Pirates and with Great Britain and France.

Answer:

_____

_____

_____

_____

_____

_____

_____

2. How did the Lewis and Clark Expedition open up the west for American immigration?

Answer:

_____

_____

_____

_____

_____

3. What were three things Jefferson did to strengthen America?

Answer:

_____

_____

_____

_____

_____

_____

_____

MAP WORK
TEST YOUR KNOWLEDGE

Practice drawing and labeling the map, until you can do so by memory.

LOUISIANA PURCHASE, 1803

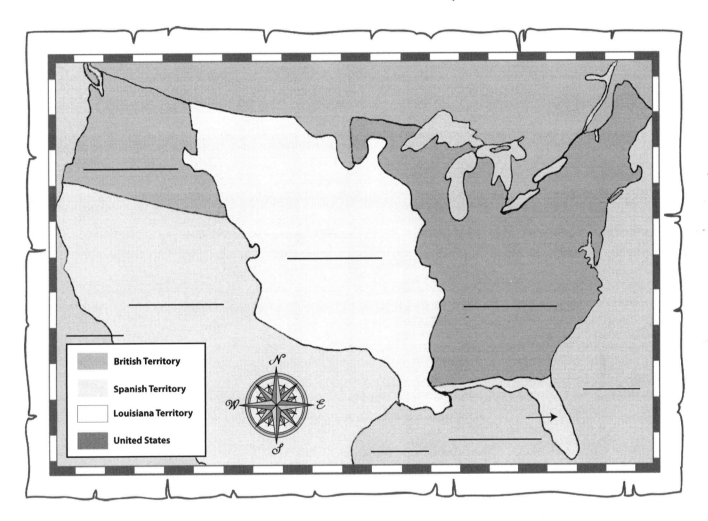

Answer these questions and test your map knowledge.

1. Approximately how much did the Louisiana Purchase expand the U.S.A? _____

2. Which country controlled the Southwest in 1803? _____

3. Which country controlled the Northwest in 1803? _____

4. After 1803, which country controlled most of what became the U.S.A? _____

5. Who controlled Florida in 1803? _____

WAR OF 1812

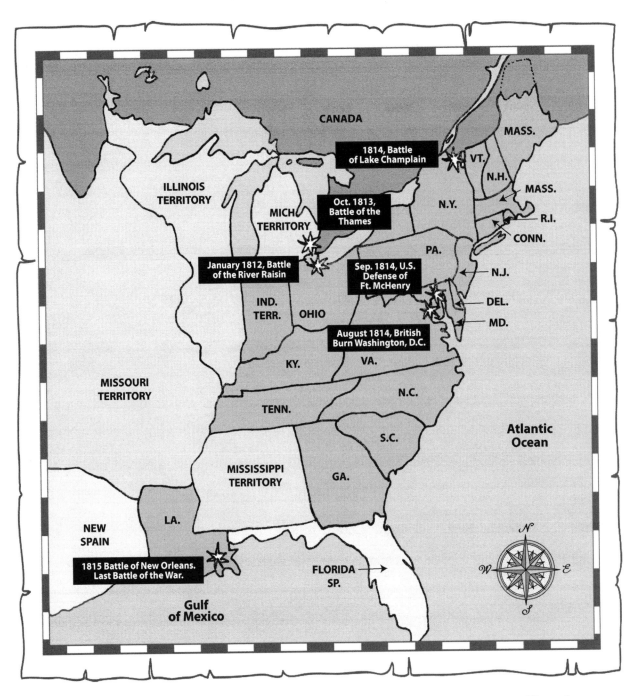

CANADA

1814, Battle of Lake Champlain

MASS.

VT.

N.H.

MASS.

ILLINOIS TERRITORY

MICH TERRITORY

Oct. 1813, Battle of the Thames

N.Y.

R.I.

CONN.

PA.

N.J.

January 1812, Battle of the River Raisin

Sep. 1814, U.S. Defense of Ft. McHenry

DEL.

IND. TERR.

OHIO

MD.

August 1814, British Burn Washington, D.C.

MISSOURI TERRITORY

KY.

VA.

TENN.

N.C.

S.C.

Atlantic Ocean

MISSISSIPPI TERRITORY

GA.

NEW SPAIN

LA.

1815 Battle of New Orleans. Last Battle of the War.

FLORIDA SP.

Gulf of Mexico

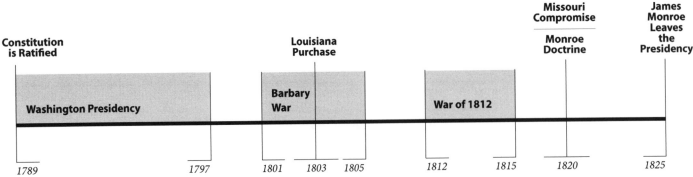

Constitution is Ratified

Washington Presidency

Louisiana Purchase

Barbary War

War of 1812

Missouri Compromise

Monroe Doctrine

James Monroe Leaves the Presidency

1789   1797   1801   1803   1805   1812   1815   1820   1825

CHAPTER 37

PRESIDENCY OF JAMES MADISON (1809-1817)

The War of 1812

James Madison

GRAMMAR
WHAT YOU NEED TO KNOW

1. **Non-intercourse Act (1809):** The Non-intercourse Act made it legal to trade with everyone except France and Great Britain. Under Jefferson, it had been illegal for Americans to trade with other countries.

2. **Macon's Bill (1810):** Macon's Bill reduced trade restrictions against Americans.

3. **Second Barbary War (1815-1816):** In the Second Barbary War, America fought and won against the Barbary Pirates.

4. **The War of 1812:** The War of 1812 was a war against Great Britain that America won. It is nicknamed "The Second American Revolution" because if Great Britain would have won, the U.S.A. could have become a colony of Great Britain again.

5. **The Battle of New Orleans (1815):** The Battle of New Orleans was America's greatest victory in the War of 1812.

6. **General Andrew Jackson:** Jackson led the Americans against the British at the Battle of New Orleans. Americans nicknamed Jackson the "Hero of New Orleans."

7. **Commodore Perry:** In the War of 1812, Commodore Perry defeated the British at the Battle of Lake Erie.

8. **The Star-Spangled Banner:** Francis Scott Key wrote this poem that became the lyrics to our

LOGIC
READING COMPREHENSION AND INFERENCE QUESTIONS

1. What can be said of the Battle of New Orleans?

      a. The British beat the Americans.

      b. It was unclear who won the battle.

      c. It was clear who won the battle.

      d. It lasted more than two months.

Answer:

Which sentence(s) best supports your answer?

_____

_____

2. Based on this lesson, you can infer the author thinks

      a. trade restrictions strengthened America in the 1800s.

      b. trade restrictions were harmful to America in the 1800s.

      c. trade restrictions had no effect on America in the 1800s.

      d. trade restrictions were the only reason America grew stronger in the 1800s.

Answer:

Which sentence(s) best supports your answer?

_____

_____

_____

_____

3. Based on the lesson, you can infer that America's military actions under Madison

      a. weakened America.

      b. had no effect on America.

      c. were seen as imperialistic.

      d. greatly strengthened America's position in the world.

Answer:

Which sentence(s) best supports your answer?

_____

_____

_____

4. Based on the lesson, you can infer the Americans

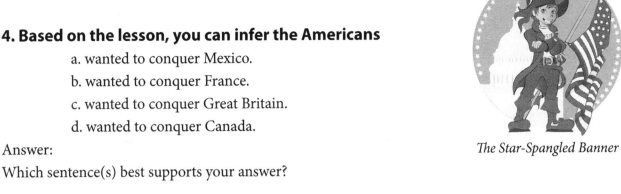

The Star-Spangled Banner

     a. wanted to conquer Mexico.

     b. wanted to conquer France.

     c. wanted to conquer Great Britain.

     d. wanted to conquer Canada.

Answer:

Which sentence(s) best supports your answer?

_____

_____

5. Which word would best describe the American victory over Great Britain in the War of 1812?

     a. standstill

     b. landslide

     c. pivotal

     d. close

Answer:

Which sentence(s) best supports this answer?

_____

_____

RHETORIC
SHORT ANSWER QUESTIONS

Answer the following with a short essay (3-5 sentences):

1. To answer this question, you will need to refer to chapters 36 and 37. How did the United States policy of dealing with people who attack and enslave Americans change from the beginning of the country through the Presidency of James Madison?

Answer:

_____

_____

_____

_____

_____

2. How did Madison's policies and Congress' laws change Jefferson's trade policy? What effect did this have on the American economy?

Answer:

_____

_____

_____

_____

_____

3. Did the United States of America benefit from the War of 1812?

Answer:

_____

_____

_____

_____

_____

_____

_____

Practice drawing and labeling the map, until you can do so by memory.

WAR OF 1812

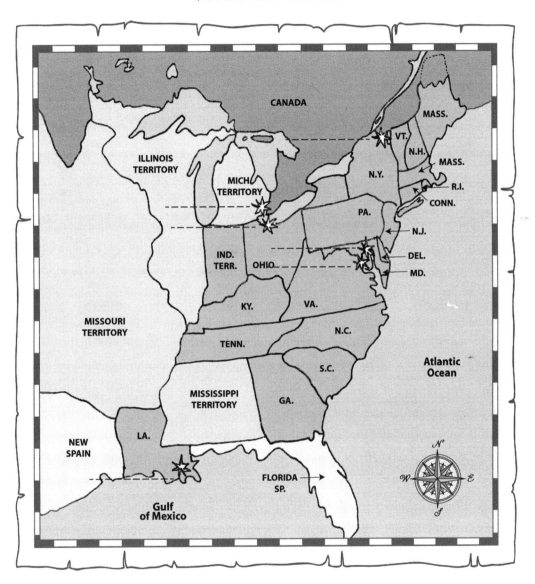

Answer these questions and test your knowledge.

1. In which state was the Star-Spangled Banner written? _____

2. Which was the last battle of the War of 1812? _____

3. During the War of 1812, who controlled Florida? _____

4. In the War of 1812, who was President? _____

5. Which body of water is south of New Orleans? _____

PRESIDENCY OF JAMES MADISON (1809-1817)   **273**

THE MONROE DOCTRINE, 1820

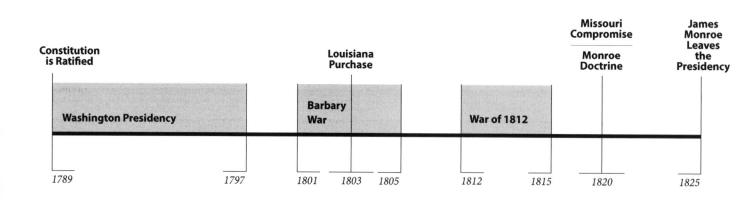

CHAPTER 38

THE ERA OF GOOD FEELINGS

James Monroe

GRAMMAR
WHAT YOU NEED TO KNOW

1. Laissez-faire: Laissez-faire is a French phrase which means a policy of hands off, limited government and minimal taxes. It was the economic policy of the United States government in the 1800s and it brought great economic growth.

2. James Monroe: Monroe was the last Founding Father as President and a traditionalist. He was the last President to wear his hair in a ponytail. He followed a policy of limited government.

3. Strict constructionist: A strict constructionist is a person who thinks the government only has power to do what is explicitly written in the Constitution. Monroe was a strict constructionist.

4. The Monroe Doctrine: In 1820, James Monroe issued a policy that forbade European countries the right to meddle in the affairs of Northern or Southern America.

5. Adams-Onis Treaty: In 1819, the U.S. bought Florida from Spain for $5 million.

LOGIC
READING COMPREHENSION AND INFERENCE QUESTIONS

1. Based on the lesson, you can infer that in the 1800s

    a. Americans were some of the poorest people in the world.

    b. Americans made state of the art tools.

    c. Americans had a problem with obesity.

    d. American students never complained.

Answer:

Which sentence(s) best supports this answer?

_____

_____

2. Based on the lesson, the American Founding Fathers

    a. succeeded in most things but failed in one main thing.

    b. succeeded in all things.

    c. failed in all things.

    d. failed in most things but succeeded in one thing.

Answer:

Which sentence(s) best supports this answer?

_____

_____

_____

_____

3. Based on the lesson, you can infer that in the early 1800s, Americans believed that a man having a ponytail was

    a. liberal

    b. feminine

    c. respectful of tradition

    d. a radical

Answer:

Which sentence(s) best supports your answer?

_____

_____

4. Based on the lesson, the Monroe Doctrine

      a. kicked the French out of South America.

      b. kicked the Spanish out of South of America.

      c. brought the United States and Great Britain closer.

      d. brought the United States and Great Britain further from each other.

Answer:

Which sentence(s) best supports this answer?

_____

_____

5. President Monroe was

      a. against using tax money for uses not specified in the Constitution.

      b. for using tax money for uses not specified in the Constitution.

      c. against using his money for uses not specified in the Constitution.

      d. for using his money as specified in the Constitution.

Answer:

Which sentence best supports this answer?

_____

_____

_____

_____

RHETORIC
SHORT ANSWER QUESTIONS

Answer the following with a short essay (3-5 sentences):

1. In chapter 41, you will find the answer to this question. It deals with the Missouri Compromise, which occurred during the Presidency of James Monroe. What were three main points of the Missouri Compromise?

Answer:

_____

_____

_____

2. Based on the lesson, what was one of the main reasons America experienced rapid economic growth in the 1800s?

Answer:

_____

_____

_____

_____

_____

3. President Monroe vetoed a bill that would have funded improvement of the Cumberland Road, even though he thought it was a good idea. Why did he reject the bill, and what does his rejection of the bill tell you about his character?

Answer:

_____

_____

_____

_____

_____

THE MONROE DOCTRINE, 1820

Answer these questions and test your knowledge.

1. **What is "Uncle Sam" pointing to?** _____

2. **Why is the Monroe Doctrine written as a line?** _____

3. **Who is opposite of Uncle Sam?** _____

4. **Which of the three figures appears in charge?** _____

5. **Which of the three looks most militaristic?** _____

American Labor Force in Agriculture, 1800 - 1860

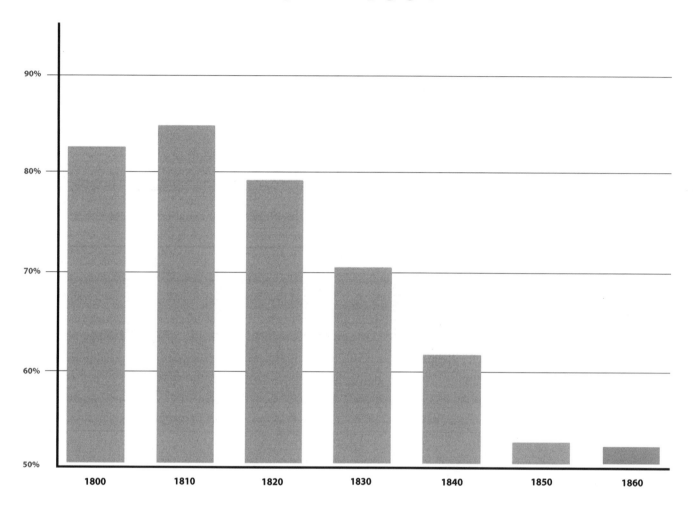

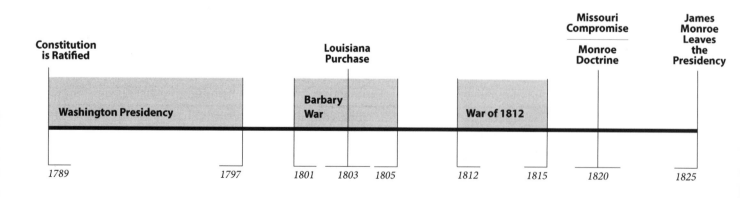

CHAPTER 39

AMERICAN SPIRIT AND INDUSTRY IN THE FREE NORTH

Cotton Gin

GRAMMAR
WHAT YOU NEED TO KNOW

1. **Industrialists:** Industrialists were men, like Andrew Carnegie, J.P. Morgan, John D. Rockefeller, and Levi Strauss, who worked hard and took risks to become successful businessmen.

2. **John Deere:** John Deere developed some of the world's finest farm products.

3. **Cyrus McCormick:** Cyrus McCormick invented the McCormick mechanical reaper, which made it easier to cut grain crops.

3. **Eli Whitney:** Eli Whitney invented the Cotton Gin, which made it easier to harvest cotton.

4. **Samuel F. B. Morse:** Samuel F.B. Morse invented the wire telegraph, which made communication over long distances easier and faster.

5. **Erie Canal:** The Erie Canal was an artificial river that connected the Great Lakes to the Hudson River and New York City.

6. **Cornelius Vanderbilt:** Cornelius Vanderbilt used steam technology and business intelligence to cut travel time and travel cost on land and sea.

LOGIC
READING COMPREHENSION AND INFERENCE QUESTIONS

1. Based on the lesson, you can infer that in the 1800s America

        a. was a land of great opportunity for all.

        b. was a land of no opportunity for all.

        c. was a land of great opportunity for all in the north.

        d. was a land of great opportunity for all in the south.

Answer:

Which sentence(s) best supports this answer?

_____

_____

_____

2. What was not one reason Americans experienced rapid economic gain and material advancement in the 1800s?

        a. abundant land

        b. scarce labor

        c. active government

        d. limited government

Answer:

Which sentence(s) best supports this answer?

_____

_____

_____

3. If you wanted someone to explain how best to build a small factory that runs on water power, which of the following would be most qualified?

        a. Charles Lane

        b. Samuel Slater

        c. Samuel F.B. Morse

        d. James Oliver

Answer:

Which sentence(s) best supports this answer?

_____

4. If you wanted to hire someone to invent machinery or farm products, where would you have the best chance of finding the most qualified person?

     a. North

     b. South

     c. East

     d. West

Answer:

Which sentence(s) best supports this answer?

_____

_____

_____

5. If you wanted to build a dormitory for laborers, who would most likely be the best person to advise you?

     a. Samuel F.B. Morse

     b. Gail Borden

     c. Eli Whitney

     d. Francis Cabot Lowell

Answer:

Which sentence(s) best supports this answer?

_____

_____

RHETORIC
SHORT ANSWER QUESTIONS

Answer the following with a short essay (3-5 sentences):

1. Based on your knowledge of geography and this lesson, why did New York City become the business capital of the country?

Answer:

_____

_____

_____

_____

_____

_____

2. Why did most of America's inventions occur in the North in the 1800s?

Answer:

_____

_____

_____

_____

_____

_____

_____

_____

3. From the inventions that are listed in this chapter, which one do you think was most beneficial to man?

Answer:

_____

_____

_____

_____

AMERICAN LABOR FORCE IN AGRICULTURE, 1800 - 1860

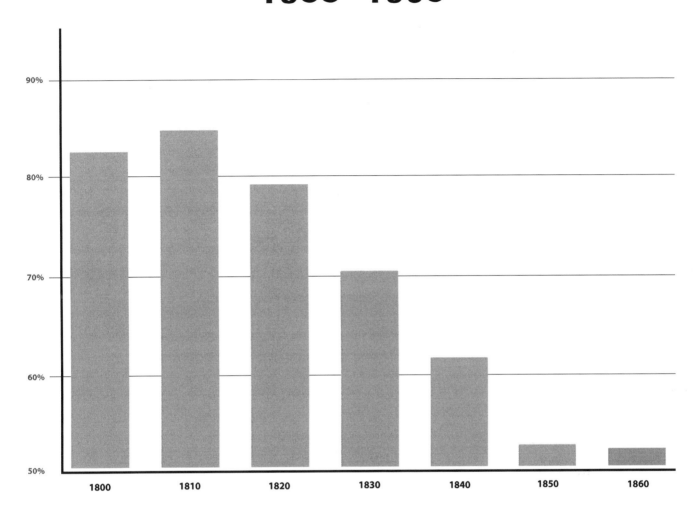

Answer these questions and test your knowledge.

1. From 1800 to 1860, which year saw the greatest number of agricultural laborers? _____

2. From 1800 to 1860, did the number of agricultural workers decrease or increase? _____

3. What was the first year the number of agricultural workers dropped below 60%?_____

4. From 1800 to 1860, which year had the lowest number of agricultural workers? _____

5. Does this chart explain at least one reason for the decrease in agricultural workers? _____

RAILROAD TRACKS, 1860

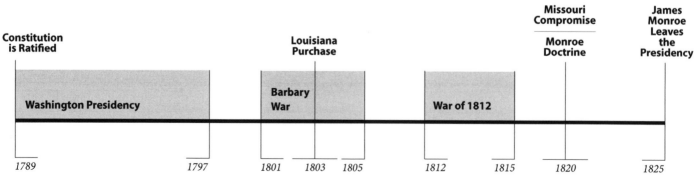

       UNIT 6: ERA OF THE FOUNDING FATHERS, 1787-1825

CHAPTER 40

RAILROADS, THE POST OFFICE, AND THE POLITICIZATION OF NEWS

Steam Engine Train

GRAMMAR
WHAT YOU NEED TO KNOW

1. Franking: Franking means the free postal privileges that American politicians enjoy.

2. Incumbent: An incumbent is an elected official. The word incumbent is often used when explaining that an official is running for office.

3. Postmaster: The Postmaster is the Head of the Post Office.

4. Baltimore to Ohio Line: In 1828, the Baltimore to Ohio railroad line was the first commercially successful railroad line in the country.

5. Transportation Revolution: In the 1800s, Americans revolutionized travel by steam technology and by business intelligence.

6. 1840 American Industry: By 1840, America led the world in ship building, iron manufacturing, publishing, and textile manufacturing.

7. The Pony Express: Between 1860 and 1861, Americans sent mail on the Pony Express, a system in which horse riders carried mail across much of the West.

1. What ended "The Canal Era?"

      a. government

      b. steam-powered railroad

      c. automobile

      d. airplane

Answer:

Which sentence(s) best supports this answer?

_____

_____

_____

2. In the United States of America, did the government or private companies do more to establish time zones and build railroad lines?

      a. government

      b. private companies

Answer:

Which sentence(s) best supports this answer?

_____

_____

_____

3. Based on the lesson, which country was most likely the leader in industrial production before 1840?

      a. U.S.A.

      b. France

      c. Russia

      d. Great Britain

Answer:

Which sentence(s) best supports this answer?

_____

_____

_____

4. Based on the lesson, how could one describe the original reason for the franking privilege?

      a. dishonorable

      b. corrupt

      c. reasonable

      d. hilarious

Answer:

Which sentence(s) best supports this answer?

_____

_____

5. Based on the lesson, in the 1870s, what was the fastest means of communication from New York to California?

      a. wire telegraph

      b. railroad

      c. Pony Express

      d. airplane

Answer:

Which sentence(s) best supports this answer?

_____

_____

RHETORIC
SHORT ANSWER QUESTIONS

Answer the following with a short essay (3-5 sentences):

1. In the early 1800s, who was most responsible for the "Transportation Revolution" in America, government or private industry?

Answer:

_____

_____

_____

_____

2. Explain one unintended consequence of the Founders establishing the franking privilege.

Answer:

_____

_____

_____

_____

3. Why did Americans tend to read more newspapers than books, when compared to Europeans, in the 1800s?

Answer:

_____

_____

_____

_____

_____

RAILROAD TRACKS, 1860

Map labels:
Portland, Boston, Buffalo, New York, La Crosse, Milwaukee, Detroit, Prairie du Chien, Pittsburgh, Philadelphia, Chicago, Baltimore, Washington D.C., Kansas City, St. Louis, Loiusville, Richmond, Atlantic Ocean, Chattanooga, Memphis, Wilmington, Atlanta, Charleston, Savannah, Mobile, Jacksonville, Houston, New Orleans, Gulf of Mexico

Answer these questions and test your map knowledge.

1. Which part of the country had more railroad tracks, the East or West? _____

2. Which part of the country had more railroad tracks, the North or the South? _____

3. Which part of the country most likely had more manufacturing, North or South? _____

4. Which part of the country most likely had a weaker transportation system, North or South?

_____

5. In 1860, were there any tracks west of Kansas City or Houston? _____

Missouri Compromise

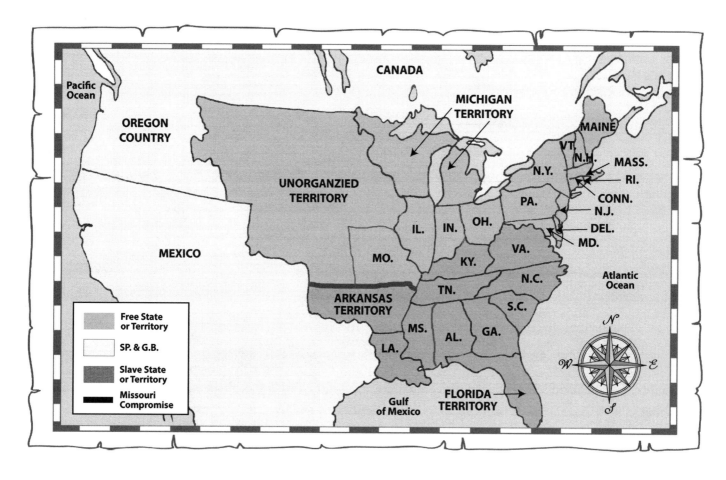

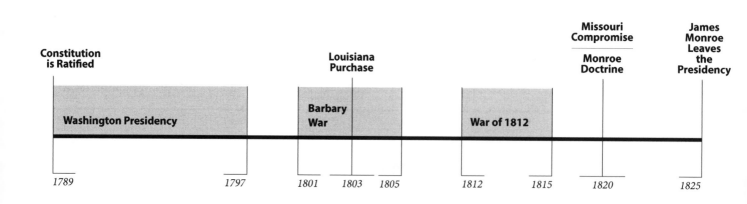

CHAPTER 41

THE MISSOURI COMPROMISE

GRAMMAR
WHAT YOU NEED TO KNOW

1. The Missouri Compromise:

    a. Missouri entered as a slave state.

    b. Maine entered as a free state.

    c. Throughout the rest of the Louisiana Territory, there would be no slavery north of the parallel 36°30', except within Missouri.

2. Fire bell in the night: This is a story where it is said Jefferson woke up and heard a fire bell in the night. It meant that Jefferson saw the slavery dilemma as if it were a fire, threatening to destroy everything.

LOGIC
READING COMPREHENSION AND INFERENCE QUESTIONS

1. Based on the lesson, you can infer that the original Americans

      a. treated the new Americans with condescension.

      b. treated the new Americans with exceptionalism.

      c. treated the new Americans very unfairly.

      d. treated the new Americans fairly.

Answer:

Which sentence(s) best supports the answer?

_____

_____

_____

2. Based on the lesson, you can infer that the American Founding Fathers

      a. solved every issue of the new republic.

      b. didn't solve many issues of the new republic.

      c. didn't solve at least one problem of the young republic.

      d. especially solved the main problem of the young republic.

Answer:

Which sentence(s) best supports the answer?

_____

_____

_____

3. Based on the lesson, you can infer the Louisiana Territory

      a. caused serious problems for America.

      b. resolved the issue of slavery for America.

      c. enabled the North and South to fight each other.

      d. enabled the North and South to resolve all of their problems.

Answer:

Which sentence(s) best supports the answer?

_____

_____

_____

4. Based on the map of the Missouri Compromise, most of the Louisiana Territory would be

      a. free

      b. slave

      c. free or slave

      d. free and slave

Answer:

5. Based on the lesson, in 1819, most Americans

      a. were in favor of slavery.

      b. were against slavery.

      c. were divided about slavery.

      d. owned slaves.

Answer:

Which sentence(s) best supports the answer?

_____

_____

_____

RHETORIC
SHORT ANSWER QUESTIONS

Answer the following with a short essay (3-5 sentences):

1. How do the rights of the new states added to the United States of America, from 1789-1821, show American Exceptionalism?

Answer:

_____

_____

_____

_____

_____

_____

_____

2. By the early 1800s, explain how America was a story of two separate countries.

Answer:

_____

_____

_____

_____

_____

3. What does the "fire bell in the night" story teach us?

Answer:

_____

_____

_____

_____

_____

MAP WORK
TEST YOUR KNOWLEDGE

Practice drawing and labeling the map, until you can do so by memory.

MISSOURI COMPROMISE

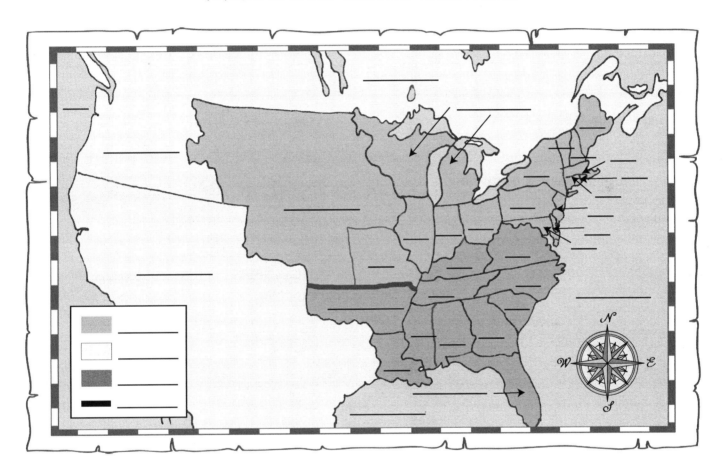

Answer these questions and test your map knowledge.

1. In the Missouri Compromise, would the area above the Missouri Compromise line be free or slave?

_____

2. Did the Missouri Compromise have anything to do with the land Mexico controlled? _____

3. In the Missouri Compromise, was Maine admitted as a slave or as a free state? _____

4. In the Missouri Compromise, was Missouri admitted as a slave or as a free state? _____

5. What does the Missouri Compromise line on the map signify? _____

_____

ACTIVITIES
UNIT 6

TOOLS OF THE HISTORIAN

COUNTERARGUMENT

In history many historians have different judgments based on the same evidence. For example, some historians view Thomas Jefferson as a hero, but there are some who think he was self-centered. These are two very different judgments on our third president. Another name for this may be perspective.
A **PERSPECTIVE** is a particular way of looking at an historical event.

When you defend your thesis statement, you should include at least one counterargument. A counterargument is an argument in which the writer presents an idea that goes against his own thesis statement. Then, in that paragraph, the writer shows how this idea is wrong.

For example, if the thesis statement to an essay was the following, "Thomas Jefferson was greatly responsible for the founding of the U.S.A.," the counterargument could look like this:

Some historians say that Thomas Jefferson was not greatly responsible for the founding of the United States. They argue this because Jefferson did not even fight in the American Revolution. These historians couldn't be more wrong. Even though Jefferson didn't raise a rifle in the war, his pen was mightier than the sword. In writing the Declaration of Independence, he let Great Britain know the reasons why Americans were fighting. Jefferson also inspired Americans to fight for high ideals. "All men are created equal" are words Americans thought of when they went into battle. "Life, liberty, and the pursuit of happiness" are words Jefferson used to make known that Americans believed each man to be entitled to rights never before granted to all people. Partly because of Jefferson's words, Americans fought bravely for many years to beat the British. Jefferson played a significant role in the American Revolution and was greatly responsible for the founding of the United States.

Notice that the beginning of this paragraph begins with the words "Some historians say." This is because you are presenting an idea that is opposite of yours. In your paragraph, be clear that you think these people are wrong.

REVISING

After writing the rough draft, it is necessary to revise. Revising involves four steps. Take your essay and perform these four tasks with a red pen in hand.

STEP I · DELETION

Delete: the end, every, just, nice, great, bad, got, everything, getting,

dead words: so, well, a lot, lots, get, good, some, yours, you, your, very

STEP II · ADDITION

A. Add words, facts, or better descriptions. Imagine you are writing for an adult who does not know the subject well. Explain every point precisely.

B. Use transitions whenever helpful.

To add ideas
further, furthermore, moreover, in addition
To show results
therefore, consequently, as a result
To indicate order
first, second, in addition to

To summarize
to sum up, to summarize, in short
To compare
similarly, likewise, by comparison
Conclusion
in conclusion, to conclude, finally

STEP III · SUBSTITUTION

Substitute repetitive or weak words.

A. Underline the first word in each sentence. If the words are the same, change some of the words.

B. Read your thesis, topic sentences, closers, and conclusion; change words as needed. Is your word choice powerful and effective? Will your essay convince the reader?

STEP IV · REARRANGEMENT

Write sentences that have a variety of beginnings.

Adjective beginnings
Well-equipped, dedicated Union soldiers
won the American Civil War.
"ing" words
Riding horses was common among
most 1800s Americans.
Prepositional phrases
Over the vast Pacific Ocean,
Columbus sailed.

Dependent clause
Because of Lincoln, the North
did not give up the war effort.
"ly" words
Bravely, Washington led the
Continental Army to victory.
Adverbs
Slowly, but surely, Grant moved
the Union Army

TYPING GUIDELINES

1. All final research papers must be typed. The Works Cited page must also be typed.
2. The font must be a standard typeface and style. Courier, Helvetica, and Times New Roman are good choices. Do not use italics, handwriting, or anything else decorative. (except italics for book titles or names of ships)
3. The size of the letters must be 12 points.
4. All margins must be one inch from the top, bottom, and each side.
5. All sentences will be double-spaced.
6. Pages will be numbered in the lower right-hand side of the page. Do not number your Cover page. The Works Cited page is numbered but does not count as a text page.

THE COVER PAGE

The Cover page needs to have the title of your research paper centered. It can be at the top, the middle, or the bottom of the page. You need to make an illustration by drawing in pencil, coloring in colored pencils, or using any other teacher-approved medium.

In the bottom right-hand corner, write or type your name, date, and period of your history teacher.

RHETORIC

THE U.S. AS A YOUNG NATION

CHALLENGES

Introduction
From 1789 to 1825, Americans faced many challenges to their new country. There were threats from abroad, vast areas of unknown land, friendly and hostile neighbors, new industries to learn, and a new government to run.

Question
Based on the evidence, what were the three greatest challenges to the young nation? Below is a list of terms and people with which you may work. You do not have to include all in your essay.

Indians	**Washington**	**Alien and Sedition Act**	**moving west**
Louisiana	**Spain**	**Jefferson**	**Hamilton**
Monroe	**Madison**	**War of 1812**	**Whiskey Rebellion**
Shay's Rebellion			

A. TAKING NOTES

Follow the structure below to write notes. Use a variety of sources.

Louisiana

What? _____

Who? _____

When? _____

Where? _____

Why? _____

Any other information? _____

_____

How much of a challenge did this present to the young republic? _____

_____

Source and page(s): _____

_____

_____

_____

B. RATING THE CONTRIBUTIONS

On the chart below write the challenge on the left, describe the challenge in the middle, and rate the challenge on the far right. A rating of 1 would be the toughest challenge and 10 the easiest.

CHALLENGE	**BRIEF DESCRIPTION**	**RATING**
1. _____	1. _____	_____
2. _____	2. _____	_____
3. _____	3. _____	_____
4. _____	4. _____	_____
5. _____	5. _____	_____
6. _____	6. _____	_____
7. _____	7. _____	_____
8. _____	8. _____	_____
9. _____	9. _____	_____
10. _____	10. _____	_____
11. _____	11. _____	_____
12. _____	12. _____	_____
13. _____	13. _____	_____
14. _____	14. _____	_____
15. _____	15. _____	_____

C. DISCUSSION

When you share ideas with others, your ideas may be reinforced, rejected, or slightly changed. Listening to your classmates' ideas will help you form your own judgment. Likewise, if you are alone in a classroom or if you are learning with your teacher, it is important that you prepare all sides of an argument. Try to learn all sides of an argument and be prepared to defend all sides.

If you are in a classroom, each student should interview at least three classmates who do not sit next to one another. If you are in a classroom with one student, then the student needs to be able to argue both or many sides to one question. The answers to the following questions must be written down on a piece of paper.

1. BASED ON THE EVIDENCE, WHAT WERE THE THREE GREATEST CHALLENGES TO THE YOUNG NATION?

2. WHY DO YOU THINK THIS?/ WHAT IS YOUR EVIDENCE?

Student 1: _____

_____

Student 2: _____

_____

Student 3: _____

_____

REFLECTION

After you have written down all your classmates' responses, think about them and ask yourself the following questions. Write down your answers under your classmates' responses.

1. WHAT DO I THINK OF THESE CLASSMATES' ANSWERS? _____

_____

2. WHICH ARE THE THREE BEST ANSWERS? _____

_____

3. HAVE I CHANGED THE WAY I THINK? HOW? _____

_____

You should now have a chance to present your ideas in a class discussion. If somebody says something with which you disagree, speak up! In your discussion, you may find out he is actually right and you are wrong. All possible viewpoints should be stated and defended out loud. Test your ideas in class.

ELECTION OF 1824 - ELECTORAL VOTES

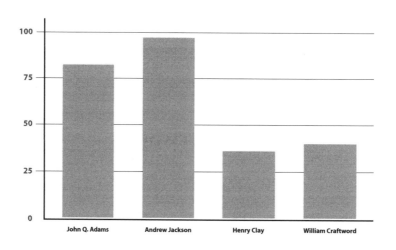

ELECTION OF 1824 - POPULAR VOTES

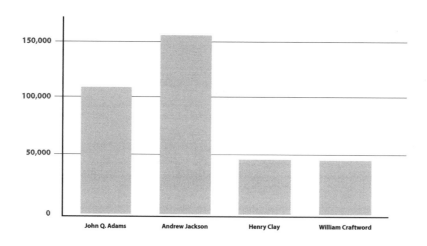

CHAPTER 42

THE ELECTION OF 1824 AND THE PRESIDENCY OF JOHN QUINCY ADAMS

John Quincy Adams

GRAMMAR
WHAT YOU NEED TO KNOW

1. **Election of 1824:** Andrew Jackson won more electoral and popular votes than any other candidate, but he did not win over 50% of either. The House of Representatives then chose John Quincy Adams the President.

2. **Corrupt Bargain:** Andrew Jackson claimed that John Quincy Adams made a deal with Speaker of the House Henry Clay: make Adams President and Clay would become Secretary of State.

3. **1825-1829:** The Presidency of John Quincy Adams was very unpopular.

4. **Popular Vote:** The popular vote means the number of people who vote.

5. **Electoral Vote:** The electoral vote is determined by the number of people in a state. Electoral votes are votes by the states. A person needs to win the electoral vote to become President.

1. Based on the lesson, you can infer that President John Quincy Adams

    a. was very likeable.

    b. was amiable.

    c. loved to get into fights.

    d. lacked interpersonal skills.

Answer:

Which sentence(s) best supports this answer?

_____

_____

2. Based on the lesson, you can infer that

    a. Adams, without doubt, made a corrupt bargain with Clay.

    b. in politics, what is believed can be more important than the truth.

    c. Jackson, without doubt, made a corrupt bargain with Adams.

    d. Clay, without doubt, made a corrupt bargain with Jackson.

Answer:

Which sentence(s) best supports this answer?

_____

_____

_____

3. What was one possible result of the Adams' Presidency?

    a. Americans never trusted Clay again.

    b. The Democratic Party chose Jackson as its first Presidential candidate.

    c. The Republicans chose Abraham Lincoln as their Presidential candidate.

    d. Jackson ran against Lincoln for the Presidency.

Answer:

Which sentence(s) best supports this question?

_____

_____

_____

RHETORIC
SHORT ANSWER QUESTIONS

Answer the following with a short essay (3-5 sentences):

1. Even though Jackson won the popular vote in 1824, why didn't he become President?

Answer:

_____

_____

_____

_____

_____

_____

_____

_____

_____

_____

2. Why did many Americans believe that Clay made a "Corrupt Bargain" with Adams?

Answer:

_____

_____

_____

_____

_____

_____

_____

_____

_____

ELECTION OF 1824 - ELECTORAL VOTES

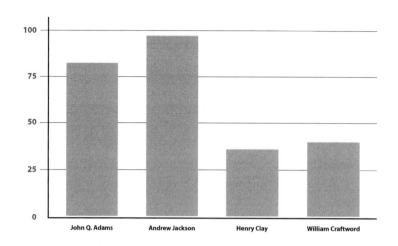

ELECTION OF 1824 - POPULAR VOTES

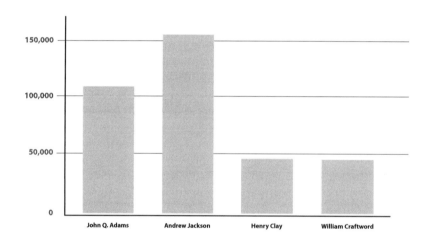

Answer these questions and test your knowledge.

1. In the election of 1824, who won the electoral vote? _____

2. In the election of 1824, who won the popular vote? _____

3. Which candidate came closest to Jackson in the electoral vote? _____

4. Which two candidates captured 3rd and 4th place in the popular and electoral votes?

_____

5. In the graph showing the popular votes, did any one candidate win over 50% of the vote total? _____

NOTES

INDIAN REMOVAL, 1830-1840

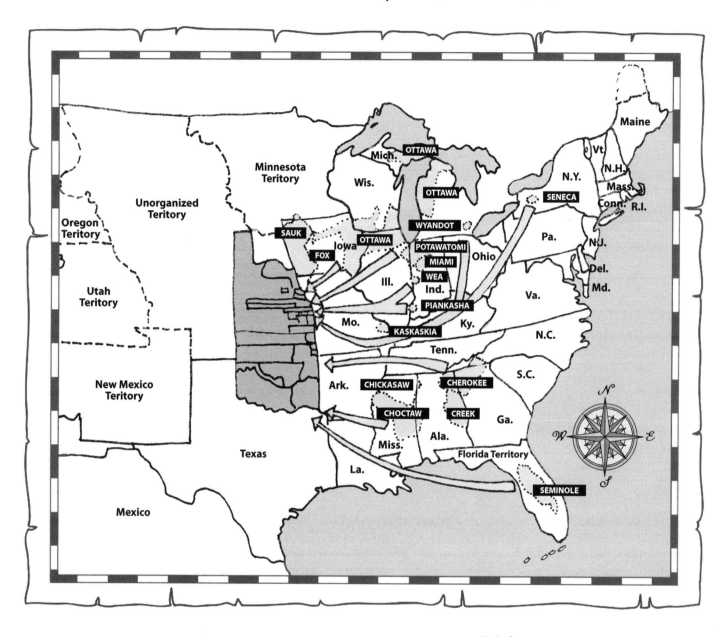

CHAPTER 43

THE AGE OF JACKSON, 1828-1836

Andrew Jackson's Log Cabin

GRAMMAR
WHAT YOU NEED TO KNOW

1. Andrew Jackson and the Democrats: Jackson is the first President of the modern Democratic Party.

2. The Spoils System: The Spoils System refers to the practice of President Jackson giving his supporters jobs.

3. Jacksonian Democracy: During Jackson's Presidency, voting rights spread to all adult white males. Before, a citizen had to own property to vote. This was an expansion of democracy.

4. Kitchen Cabinet: Jackson trusted a few loyal advisors, known as his Kitchen Cabinet, as if they met in the kitchen.

5. Cherokee Indians: Americans called the Cherokee the "civilized tribe" because they adopted Christianity, had a written language, and adopted Western ways.

6. Indian Removal Act: This 1830 law allowed the federal government to use force to help remove Indians only when they agreed to leave their land.

7. Trail of Tears: Presidents Jackson and Van Buren ordered the American military to forcefully remove 20,000 Indians west of the Mississippi. Over 3,000 died on the forced march. Jackson and Van Buren violated the Constitution with these orders.

8. Internal Improvements: Jackson broke with tradition and spent more money on roads and harbors than all other Presidents combined.

9. Nullification Crisis: South Carolina wanted to nullify a law. Jackson threatened use of the military to force South Carolina to follow the law. A compromise was reached.

10. Jackson's War on the Bank: Jackson wanted to replace the leadership of the U.S. Bank and worked to kill the U.S. Bank, which ended in 1836.

Logic
Reading Comprehension and Inference Questions

1. Based on the lesson, you can infer the author

    a. thinks Jackson's Presidency was not all good.

    b. thinks Jackson was a great President.

    c. thinks Jackson's Presidency was all bad.

    d. thinks Jackson's Presidency loved the Constitution.

Answer:

Which sentence(s) best supports this answer?

_____

_____

2. Based on the lesson, Jackson

    a. always supported states' rights over the federal government.

    b. always supported the federal government over states' rights.

    c. always supported whatever made the Democratic Party stronger.

    d. always supported the rule of law.

Answer:

Which sentence(s) best supports this answer?

_____

_____

_____

3. What was one political issue not mentioned in the 1828 elections?

    a. trade

    b. drinking whiskey

    c. abusing slaves

    d. slavery

Answer:

Which sentence(s) best supports this answer?

_____

_____

_____

4. Place the following in chronological order:

        a. General Scott removed 12,000 Indians from Georgia

        b. 1828 election

        c. Adams' Presidency

        d. Nullification Crisis

Answer:

5. Vice President Calhoun favored, in this order:

        a. the U.S.A. over freedom

        b. freedom over the U.S.A.

        c. The U.S.A. over political rights

        d. political rights over the U.S.A.

Answer:

Which sentence(s) best supports your answer?

_____

_____

RHETORIC
SHORT ANSWER QUESTIONS

Answer the following with a short essay (3-5 sentences):

1. Why did Martin Van Buren want elections to be filled with personal political attacks and not include any discussion of slavery?

_____

_____

_____

_____

_____

2. In your opinion, did Jackson strengthen or weaken America?

Answer:

_____

_____

_____

_____

_____

_____

_____

_____

_____

3. How did the spoils system work and why is Jackson's Presidency tied closely with the Spoils System?

Answer:

_____

_____

_____

_____

_____

MAP WORK
TEST YOUR KNOWLEDGE

INDIAN REMOVAL, 1830-1840

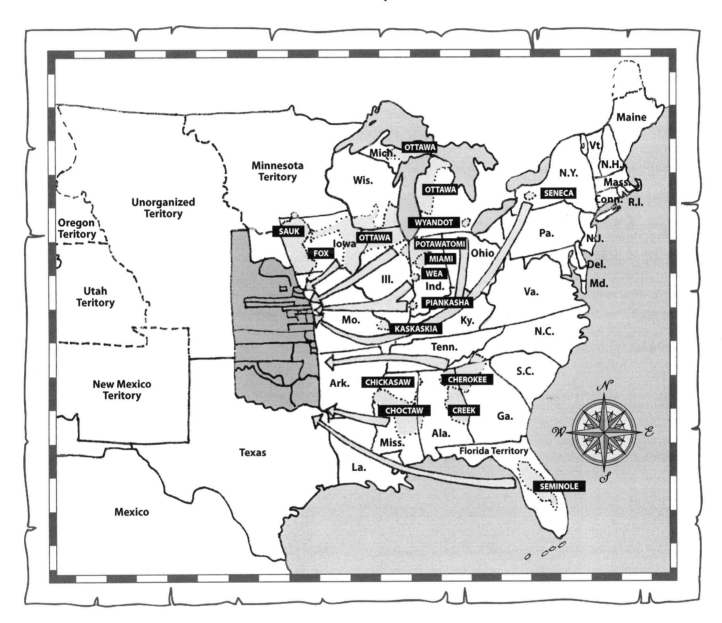

Answer these questions and test your knowledge.

1. Which direction were Indians forced to move? _____

2. Beyond which large river did Indians have to move? _____

3. From where did Indians have to move? (North, South, East, West?) _____

4. Which direction were the Indians forced to move? _____

5. Which President started to remove Indians west of the Mississippi? _____

ACTIVITIES
UNIT 7

RHETORIC
OPEN-ENDED ESSAY QUESTION

INTRODUCTION

From 1825 to 1836, the federal government expanded greatly. U.S. federal expenditures rose, government employment rose, and Presidents Andrew Jackson and Martin Van Buren used federal forces in ways that previous Presidents hadn't.

QUESTION

Did the expansion of the federal government from 1825 to 1836 weaken or strengthen the United States of America? In your answer, show in what ways the federal government expanded.

RESEARCH ACTIVITIES

A. THE POST OFFICE

For this research, the student has to go back to Chapter 40, which deals specifically with the Post Office.

1. In the first half of the 1800s, which governmental office was one of the most powerful, and why?

_____

_____

_____

2. What was franking and how did it influence the news?

_____

_____

3. Who wanted more post offices and why?

_____

_____

4. What was the stance of the federal government regarding private mail deliveries?

_____

_____

B. ANDREW JACKSON'S PRESIDENCY

1. What was the spoils system that Martin Van Buren established with the Bucktail Republicans in New York?

_____

_____

_____

2. What national political party did Martin Van Buren form?

_____

_____

3. Relative to all other Presidents, how much did Andrew Jackson spend on internal improvements?

_____

_____

4. Explain the Force Act of 1833.

_____

_____

5. How did U.S. federal expenditures rise with the Presidency of Andrew Jackson?

_____

_____

6. In what ways did President Jackson and President Van Buren expand the power of the federal government in their removal of American Indians west of the Mississippi?

_____

_____

_____

_____

C. DISCUSSION

When you share ideas with others, your ideas may be reinforced, rejected, or slightly changed. Listening to your classmates' ideas will help you form your own judgment. Likewise, if you are alone in a classroom or if you are learning with your teacher, it is important that you prepare all sides of an argument. Try to learn all sides of an argument and be prepared to defend all sides.

If you are in a classroom, each student should interview at least three classmates who do not sit next to one another. If you are in a classroom with one student, then the student needs to be able to argue both or many sides to one question. The answers to the following questions must be written down on a piece of paper.

1. DID THE EXPANSION OF THE FEDERAL GOVERNMENT FROM 1825 TO 1836 WEAKEN OR STRENGTHEN THE UNITED STATES OF AMERICA? IN YOUR ANSWER, SHOW IN WHAT WAYS THE FEDERAL GOVERNMENT EXPANDED.
2. WHY DO YOU THINK THIS?/ WHAT IS YOUR EVIDENCE?

Student 1: _____

_____

Student 2: _____

_____

Student 3: _____

_____

REFLECTION

After you have written down all your classmates' responses, think about them and ask yourself the following questions. Write down your answers under your classmates' responses.

1. WHAT DO I THINK OF THESE CLASSMATES' ANSWERS? _____

_____

2. WHICH ARE THE THREE BEST ANSWERS? _____

_____

3. HAVE I CHANGED THE WAY I THINK? HOW? _____

_____

You should now have a chance to present your ideas in a class discussion. If somebody says something with which you disagree, speak up! In your discussion, you may find out he is actually right and you are wrong.

MANUFACTURING WORKERS IN THE UNITED STATES, 1850 - 1900

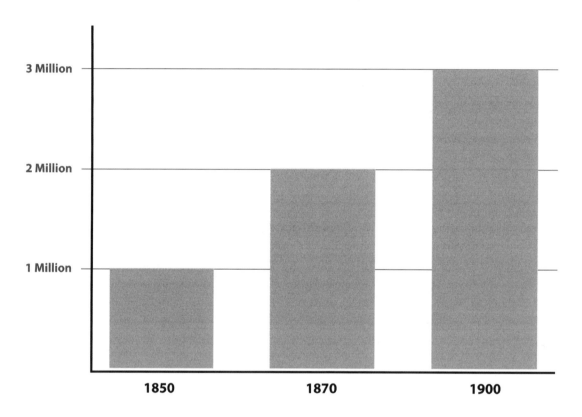

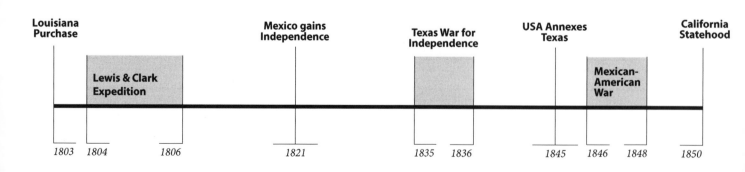

CHANGE IN AMERICA: INDUSTRIALIZATION, RELIGION, AND SOCIAL CHANGE

Susan B. Anthony   *Harriet Tubman*

GRAMMAR
WHAT YOU NEED TO KNOW

1. **Empire of Liberty:** Thomas Jefferson believed America was going to be an empire of liberty, with small farmers moving west for 1,000 years.

2. **Manifest Destiny:** Many European-Americans believed God gave them the right to conquer and inhabit the west so that America would spread to the Pacific Ocean.

3. **Industrial Revolution:** The Industrial Revolution was a societal change in how people made a living. Americans moved from being farmers to working in factories and living in cities.

4. **Second Great Awakening:** In this 1800s religious movement, Christian ministers urged Americans to get closer to Jesus. Americans formed new Protestant Christian religions.

5. **Standard of Living:** The standard of living means the economic level most citizens live in. In the 1800s, the standard of living rapidly rose for most Americans.

6. **Church of Jesus Christ of Latter Day Saints:** Known as Mormons, this new religion posited the idea that Jesus had visited America thousands of years ago.

7. **Utopia:** A utopia is an ideal of the perfect society.

8. Socialist Robert Owen: Owen tried to found a society that rejected God, marriage, and private property. His society ran out of food.

9. Shakers: The Shakers were a religious group that did not believe in procreation.

10. Amish: The Amish are a Christian group who founded their community on Christian principles and the rejection of modern conveniences, like electricity.

11. Feminism: Beginning in the 1800s, American feminism was a movement towards voting and equal rights for women.

12. Abolitionism: Abolitionism was the movement against slavery.

13. Elizabeth Cady Stanton and Susan B. Anthony: These two were important American feminists.

14. Frederick Douglass: Douglass was a runaway slave who became a leader of the abolitionist movement.

15. Harriet Tubman: Tubman was an escaped slave who helped over 70 slaves escape to freedom.

16. The Underground Railroad: The Underground Railroad was a system of safe homes and routes slaves would use to escape to freedom.

17. Washington Irving: Irving wrote "Rip Van Winkle" and "The Legend of Sleepy Hollow."

18. James Fenimore Cooper: Cooper created the western novel and wrote *The Last of the Mohicans*.

19. Herman Melville: Melville wrote *Moby Dick* and other sea-faring stories.

20. Nathaniel Hawthorne: Hawthorne wrote *The Scarlet Letter*.

21. Edgar Allen Poe: Poe created the short detective and the short horror story.

22. Henry Wadsworth Longfellow: Longfellow wrote "The Midnight Ride of Paul Revere."

23. Ralph Waldo Emerson: Emerson was a Transcendentalist poet.

24. Hudson River School: In this circle of painters, American artists painted the American landscape.

1. Based on the lesson, you can infer that

    a. America's government in the first half of the 1800s did less than other governments.

    b. America's government in the first half of the 1800s did a great deal of things.

    c. In the 1800s, immigrants received free education and free health care.

    d. In the 1800s, life was hard.

Answer:

Which sentence(s) best supports this answer?

_____

_____

2. Based on the lessons, you can infer

    a. American Christians worried a great deal about following tradition.

    b. Pub songs should never be sung in churches.

    c. Americans used creative strategies to excite people about Christianity.

    d. Most Americans were atheists.

Answer:

Which sentence(s) best supports this answer?

_____

_____

3. Based on the lesson, on which principles did commune societies succeed?

    a. communist

    b. socialist

    c. fascist

    d. Christian

Answer:

Which sentence(s) best supports this answer?

_____

_____

4. Based on the lesson, what can you infer about how the 1800s feminist would think of modern-day feminists?

      a. They are doing everything the early feminists did.

      b. Modern-day feminists are destroying what early feminists started.

      c. Modern-day feminists are wrong in their support of abortion rights.

      d. Modern-day feminists are right in their support of abortion rights.

Answer:

Which sentence(s) best supports this answer?

_____

_____

5. Based on the lesson, abolitionism was

      a. supported only by black Americans.

      b. supported by all American Founding Fathers.

      c. supported by no American Founding Fathers.

      d. supported by some American Founding Fathers.

Answer:

Which sentence(s) best supports this answer?

_____

_____

RHETORIC
SHORT ANSWER QUESTIONS

Answer the following with a short essay (3-5 sentences):

1. Were all American Founding Fathers in favor of enslaving blacks?

Answer:

_____

_____

_____

_____

2. In what ways was American literature of the 1800s new?

Answer:

_____

_____

_____

3. In relation to the world, did American women of the 1800s have more or less rights?

Answer:

_____

_____

_____

_____

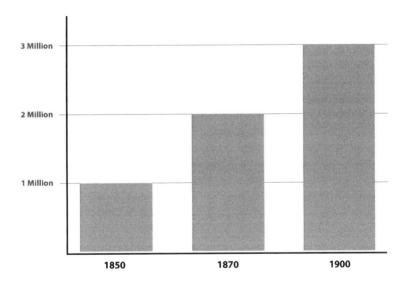

MANUFACTURING WORKERS IN THE UNITED STATES, 1850 - 1900

Answer these questions and test your knowledge.

1. In 1850, how many manufacturing workers were in the U.S.A? _____

2. In 1870, how many manufacturing workers were in the U.S.A? _____

3. In 1900, how many manufacturing workers were in the U.S.A? _____

4. From 1850 to 1900, how many more manufacturing workers were in the U.S.A? _____

5. How many times more manufacturing laborers were in the U.S.A. in 1900 than 1850? _____

AMERICAN COLLEGES
1636 - 1860

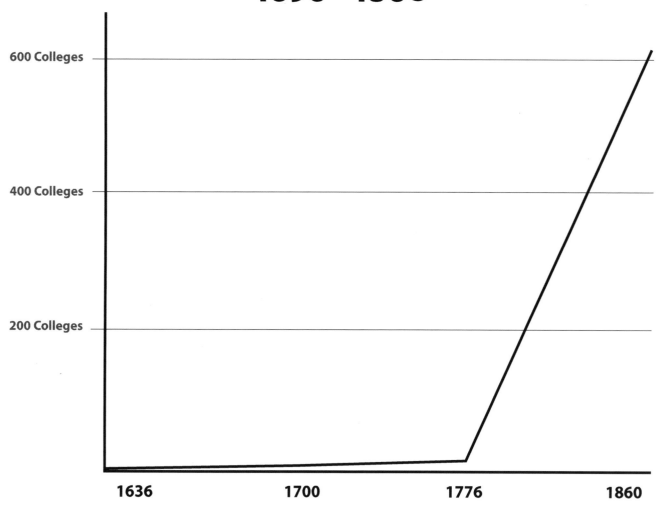

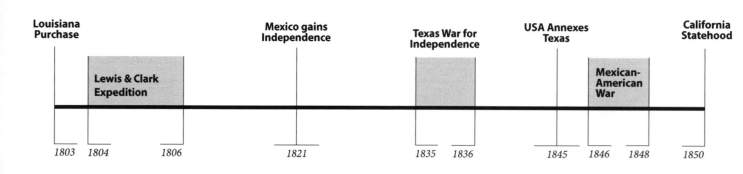

UNIT 8: EMPIRE OF LIBERTY OR MANIFEST DESTINY, 1836-1848

CHAPTER 45

EDUCATION IN EARLY AMERICA THROUGH THE CIVIL WAR

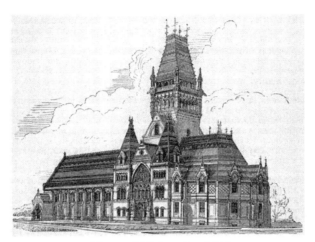

Harvard University, 1636

GRAMMAR
WHAT YOU NEED TO KNOW

1. Apprentice: An apprentice was a boy who learned a trade by living in the household and working for a master tradesman for a number of years.

2. McGuffey's Readers: These were a series of schoolbooks that taught academics and Christian morality for grades 1-6.

3. Classical Education: This educational approach among Americans focused on learning classical languages, reading great books, searching for the truth, and engaging in discussion.

4. Northwest Ordinance of 1787: This law encouraged religion and morality be taught as part of education in the Northwest territories. In the 1800s, Christian principles were taught in public universities.

5. Harvard University: Harvard was founded in 1636 as a university to train Christian ministers. Harvard is America's oldest university.

6. Horace Mann: Mann was a leading spokesman for a publicly-funded educational system that taught academic, physical, and moral values that promote democracy.

7. 1852: In 1852, Massachusetts adopted a publicly-funded educational system. Afterwad, each state established similar systems.

LOGIC
READING COMPREHENSION AND INFERENCE QUESTIONS

1. Based on the reading, you can infer that the colonists of the 1600s and 1700s were

     a. ignorant

     b. illiterate

     c. religious

     d. Muslim

Answer:

Which sentence(s) best supports this answer?

_____

_____

_____

2. If you were a 15-year-old boy in Boston, you very likely lived

     a. on a farm.

     b. on a ship.

     c. in someone else's home.

     d. under the ground.

Answer:

Which sentence(s) best supports this answer?

_____

_____

_____

3. Based on the reading, you can infer that overall literacy rate in the South relative to the North was

     a. higher

     b. lower

     c. the same

     d. nonexistent

Answer:

Which sentence(s) best supports this answer?

_____

_____

_____

4. Based on the lesson, you can infer that Europe's colleges in the 1700s and 1800s were

       a. more government-directed than America's colleges

       b. less government-directed than America's colleges

       c. the same in terms of government direction as America's colleges.

       d. just as big as America's colleges.

Answer:

Which sentence(s) best supports this answer?

_____

_____

5. Based on the lesson, you can infer that Horace Mann

       a. despised the Prussian education system.

       b. loved the Prussian education system.

       c. wanted to create a totalitarian government.

       d. wanted students to learn so they would contribute positively to a free society.

Answer:

Which sentence(s) best supports this answer?

_____

_____

RHETORIC
SHORT ANSWER QUESTIONS

Answer the following with a short essay (3-5 sentences):

1. What are the similarities between Europe's colleges and America's state-funded public school systems?

_____

_____

_____

_____

_____

_____

2. Describe the role religion played in American education of the 1600s through the early 1800s.

Answer:

_____

_____

_____

_____

_____

_____

_____

3. _The Story of Liberty_ **reports that the literacy rate in America was 97% in the mid-1800s (not considering the slave population). Research on your own what is America's literacy rate today.**

Answer:

_____

_____

AMERICAN COLLEGES
1636 - 1860

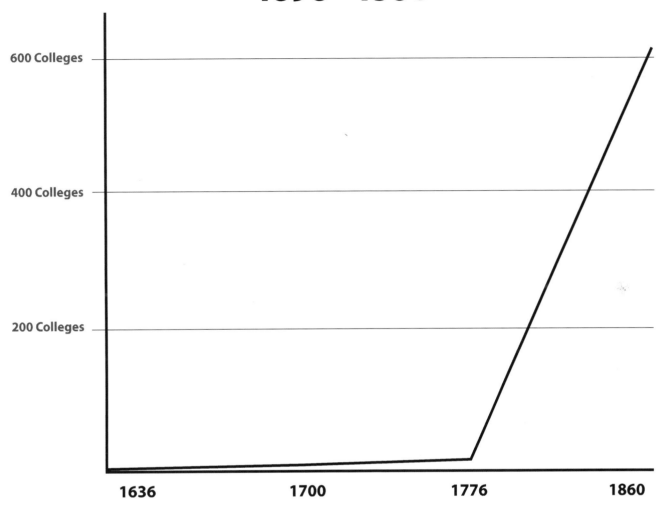

Answer these questions and test your knowledge.

1. **When was the first American college established?** _____

2. **From 1636 to 1860, how many American colleges were established?** _____

3. **From the 17th through the 19th centuries, which century saw the most American colleges established?** _____

4. **Under which government were 600 colleges established?** _____

5. **About what was the percentage growth of colleges in America from 1776 to 1860?**

_____

TEXAS WAR FOR INDEPENDENCE, 1835-1836

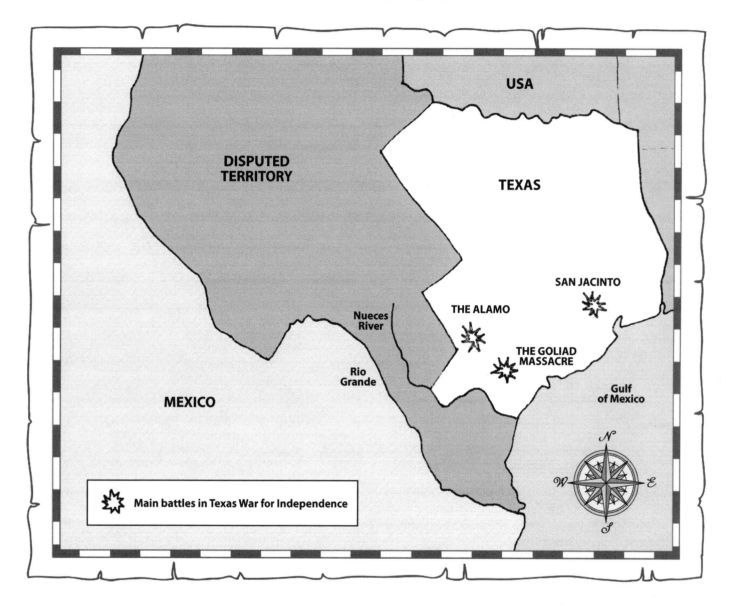

DISPUTED TERRITORY

USA

TEXAS

SAN JACINTO

THE ALAMO

THE GOLIAD MASSACRE

Nueces River

Rio Grande

MEXICO

Gulf of Mexico

Main battles in Texas War for Independence

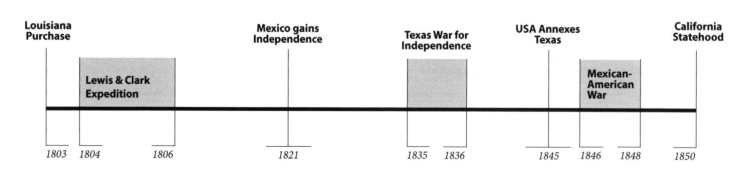

Louisiana Purchase

Lewis & Clark Expedition

Mexico gains Independence

Texas War for Independence

USA Annexes Texas

Mexican-American War

California Statehood

1803 1804   1806   1821   1835 1836   1845 1846 1848   1850

CHAPTER 46

THE SOUTHWEST AND THE WAR FOR TEXAS INDEPENDENCE (1835-1836)

Sam Houston

WHAT YOU NEED TO KNOW

1. Father Junipero Serra: Fr. Serra established Catholic missions for Spain in California.

2. 1821: In 1821, Mexico gained independence from Spain and California became a part of Mexico, which seized all Church properties.

3. War for Texas Independence: From 1835 to 1836, Texas fought Mexico for its independence.

4. Stephen Austin: Austin was Mexico's director of American immigration to Texas.

5. Sam Houston: Houston led the Texan military to defeat Mexico and Houston became a President of Texas.

6. Santa Anna: Santa Anna was the dictator of Mexico and led the Mexican Army to defeat in the Texas War for Independence.

7. Remember the Alamo: Texans would say "Remember the Alamo" to inspire each other to fight Mexico for independence.

8. Massacre at Goliad: The Mexican Army shot or clubbed and knifed to death c. 445 Texan prisoners of war.

9. Battle of San Jacinto: Texans defeated Santa Anna at this battle. Santa Anna signed a peace treaty that established Texas as a republic, with the Rio Grande River as the border between Texas and Mexico.

10. The Republic of Texas: From 1836 to 1845, Texas was an independent country.

LOGIC
READING COMPREHENSION AND INFERENCE QUESTIONS

1. Based on the lesson, you can infer that Father Serra

     a. was a complete failure.

     b. was a complete success.

     c. completely destroyed all culture in California.

     d. was a man of hatred towards the Indians.

Answer:

Which sentence(s) best supports your answer?

_____

_____

_____

2. Based on the lesson, you can infer that Mexico

     a. loved the Catholic Church.

     b. treated the Catholic Church very well.

     c. hated the Catholic Church with a passion.

     d. stole the real estate of the Catholic Church.

Answer:

Which sentence(s) best supports your answer?

_____

_____

_____

3. Based on the lesson, during the 1820s, Mexico

     a. failed to establish law and order in Texas.

     b. established law and order in Texas.

     c. agreed that the Texans could own slaves.

     d. decided to make Santa Anna their god.

Answer:

Which sentence(s) best supports your answer?

_____

_____

_____

4. Based on the lesson, you can infer that at the Alamo

      a. Mexicans did not fight bravely.

      b. Texans did not fight bravely.

      c. Santa Anna was a great, beloved military genius.

      d. Santa Anna was a poor, despised military leader.

Answer:

Which sentence(s) best supports your answer?

_____

_____

5. Place the following in chronological order:

      a. Battle of San Jacinto

      b. Texas becomes the Republic of Texas

      c. Battle of the Alamo

      d. Americans begin immigrating into Texas

Answer:

RHETORIC
SHORT ANSWER QUESTIONS

Answer the following with a short essay (3-5 sentences):

1. Was Texas justified in fighting Mexico for its independence?

_____

_____

_____

_____

_____

_____

_____

_____

_____

2. Compare the number of years Spain held Texas to the years Mexico held Texas before Texas won its independence.

Answer:

_____

_____

_____

_____

3. How did the tactics and leadership of Sam Houston and Santa Anna differ in the War for Texas Independence?

Answer:

_____

_____

_____

_____

_____

_____

_____

_____

MAP WORK
TEST YOUR KNOWLEDGE

Practice drawing and labeling the map, until you can do so by memory.

TEXAS WAR FOR INDEPENDENCE, 1835-1836

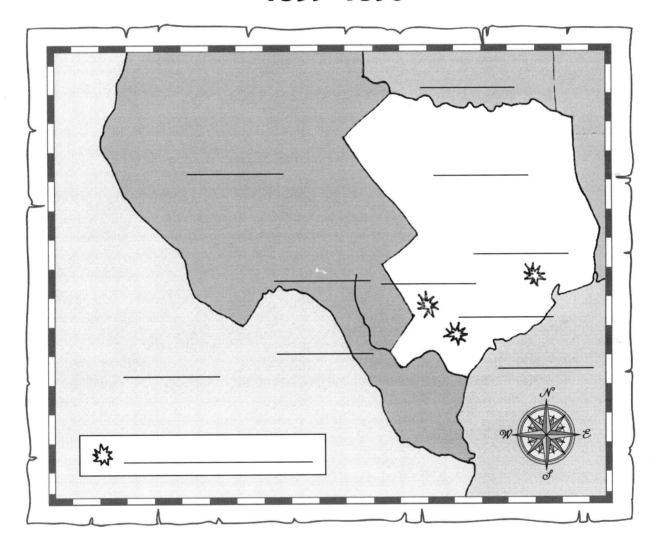

Answer these questions and test your knowledge.

1. Between which two rivers was there a land dispute? _____

2. Name a battle that resulted in a Mexican victory? _____

3. Name a battle that ended in a Texan victory? _____

4. In relation to Mexico, where is Texas? _____

5. In relation to the U.S.A., where is Texas? _____

AMERICAN POPULATION
1790 - 1860

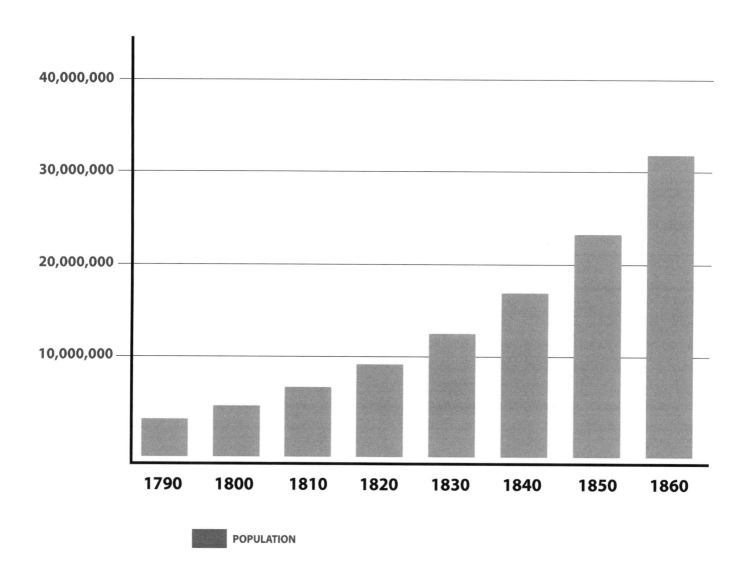

POPULATION

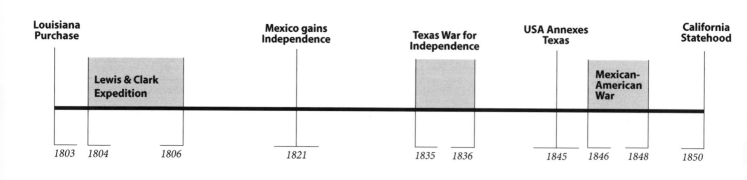

CHAPTER 47

PRESIDENCIES OF VAN BUREN (1837-1841), HARRISON (1841), AND TYLER (1841-1845)

Martin Van Buren

John Tyler

William Henry Harrison

GRAMMAR
WHAT YOU NEED TO KNOW

1. **Martin Van Buren:** Martin Van Buren was the architect of the modern Democratic Party and President from 1837 to 1841.

2. **Panic of 1837:** The Panic of 1837 was an economic depression.

3. **William Henry Harrison:** Harrison was President in 1841 for one month, caught pneumonia, and died.

4. **Battle of Tippecanoe:** General Harrison defeated the Shawnee Indians in 1811 at the Battle of Tippecanoe and became a war hero.

5. **John Tyler:** Tyler served as President from 1841 to 1845.

LOGIC
READING COMPREHENSION AND INFERENCE QUESTIONS

1. **Based on the reading, you can infer that Martin Van Buren**

      a. disagreed with Jackson on key issues.

      b. agreed with Jackson on slavery.

      c. looked like Jackson.

      d. shared the same vision of the Democratic Party as Jackson.

Answer:

Which sentence(s) best supports your answer?

_____

_____

_____

2. **Place the events in chronological order:**

      a. Tyler Presidency

      b. Jackson Presidency

      c. Van Buren Presidency

      d. Harrison Presidency

Answer:

3. **Based on the lesson, you can infer that from 1837 to 1845**

      a. Mexico had little influence on America.

      b. America had little influence on Mexico.

      c. Mexico probably had great influence on America.

      d. America definitely had great influence on Mexico.

Answer:

Which sentence(s) best supports the answer?

_____

_____

_____

RHETORIC
SHORT ANSWER QUESTIONS

Answer the following with a short essay (3-5 sentences):

1. What does William Henry Harrison's political campaign for president tell us about Americans in the 1800s?

_____

_____

_____

_____

_____

_____

_____

2. What influence did the Presidencies of Van Buren, Harrison, and Tyler have on Americans expanding westward?

_____

_____

_____

_____

_____

_____

_____

AMERICAN POPULATION
1790 - 1860

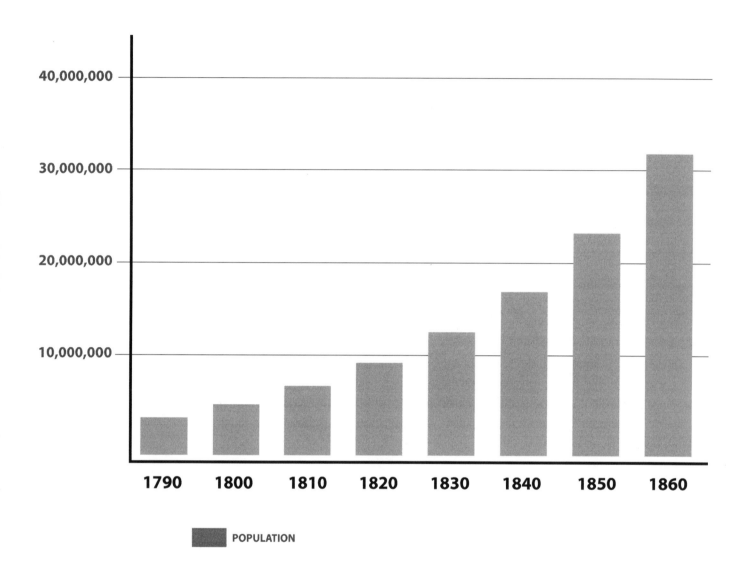

Answer these questions and test your knowledge.

1. About how many Americans were there in 1790? _____

2. About how many Americans were there in 1820? _____

3. About how many Americans were there in 1860? _____

4. About how may years did it take for the population of the United States to triple from 1790?

_____

5. From 1830, about how many years did it take for America's population to double?

_____

NOTES

MEXICAN-AMERICAN WAR, 1846-1848

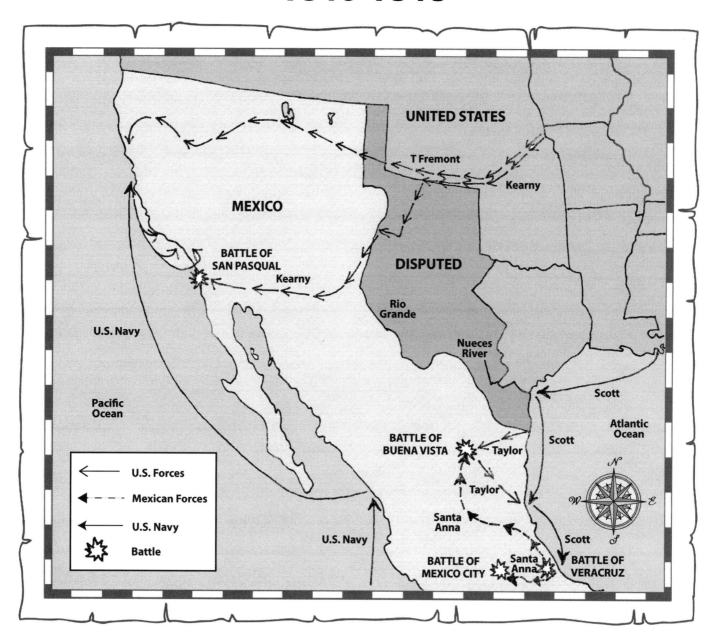

Legend:
- U.S. Forces
- Mexican Forces
- U.S. Navy
- Battle

UNITED STATES

MEXICO

DISPUTED

T Fremont

Kearny

Rio Grande

Nueces River

BATTLE OF SAN PASQUAL

Kearny

U.S. Navy

Pacific Ocean

BATTLE OF BUENA VISTA

Taylor

Scott

Atlantic Ocean

Scott

Taylor

Santa Anna

U.S. Navy

BATTLE OF MEXICO CITY

Santa Anna

Scott

BATTLE OF VERACRUZ

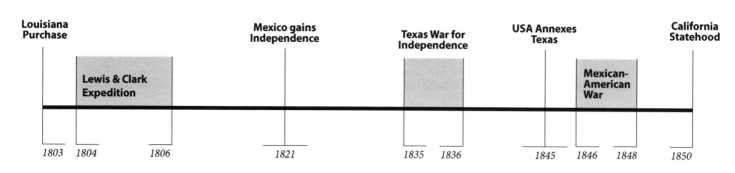

Louisiana Purchase

Lewis & Clark Expedition

Mexico gains Independence

Texas War for Independence

USA Annexes Texas

Mexican-American War

California Statehood

1803   1804   1806   1821   1835   1836   1845   1846   1848   1850

Chapter 48

Presidency of Polk (1845-1849) and the Mexican-American War (1846-1848)

Westward Expansion Map

Sam Houston

GRAMMAR
WHAT YOU NEED TO KNOW

1. James K. Polk: Polk, a Democrat, served as President from 1845 to 1849.

2. Annex: To annex means when a country acquires territory without going to war.

3. Annexation of Texas: In 1845, the U.S.A. annexed Texas.

4. Rio Grande River: Santa Anna signed a peace treaty with Texas in 1836 designating the Rio Grande as the border between the two countries. Mexico recognized the Nueces River as the border, not the Rio Grande.

5. Conscript: A conscript is a person who is forced to join the military through the draft.

6. Gringo: Gringo is a pejorative that Americans were called during the Mexican-American War.

7. Treaty of Guadalupe Hidalgo: In 1848, Mexico and the U.S.A. signed a peace treaty. America paid Mexico $15 million, and America claimed the Southwest (land that would become Arizona, New Mexico, Utah, Nevada, and California, and the disputed land in Texas).

LOGIC
READING COMPREHENSION AND INFERENCE QUESTIONS

1. Based on the reading, President Polk's policy of expansion

     a. caused the Civil War.

     b. had no influence on the Civil War.

     c. hastened the coming of the Civil War.

     d. slowed the coming of the Civil War.

Answer:

Which sentence(s) best supports the answer?

_____

_____

_____

2. Based on the lesson, you can infer that Americans in 1845

     a. were mainly anti-slavery.

     b. were mainly pro-slavery.

     c. were for making America larger.

     d. were for making America great again.

Answer:

Which sentence(s) best supports the answer?

_____

_____

_____

3. Based on the reading, you can infer that the question of admitting Texas as a state

     a. created no problems.

     b. was met with approval by all Americans.

     c. was met with approval by all Mexicans.

     d. was looked at differently by Northerners and Southerners.

Answer:

Which sentence(s) best supports the answer?

_____

_____

_____

4. Based on the lesson, you can infer that Mexico

      a. was respectful towards the Texans and Santa Anna.

      b. treated the Texans and Santa Anna with care.

      c. didn't always respect the Texans and Santa Anna.

      d. was innocent in regards to the Mexican-American War.

Answer:

Which sentence(s) best supports the answer?

_____

_____

_____

_____

5. Based on the lesson, one could argue that

      a. Many Mexicans wanted to live in Texas.

      b. No Mexican wanted to live in the Southwest.

      c. There was no reason to fight over the Mexican Cession.

      d. For every Mexican in the Southwest, 3 soldiers were fighting for him.

Answer:

Which sentence(s) best supports this answer?

_____

_____

_____

RHETORIC
SHORT ANSWER QUESTIONS

Answer the following with a short essay (3-5 sentences):

1. Before the Mexican-American War, were the Americans or the Mexicans correct in their evaluation of what the southern border of Texas was?

_____

_____

_____

_____

2. How did President Polk's successes bring the United States of America closer to a civil war?

_____

_____

_____

_____

_____

_____

3. Was the Treaty of Guadalupe Hidalgo fair?

_____

_____

_____

_____

_____

_____

_____

_____

MAP WORK
TEST YOUR KNOWLEDGE

Practice drawing and labeling the map, until you can do so by memory.

MEXICAN-AMERICAN WAR, 1846-1848

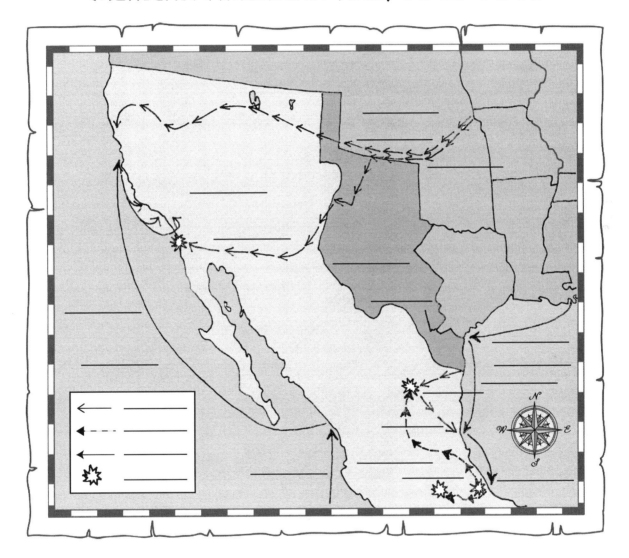

Answer these questions and test your knowledge.

1. Name one battle that resulted in an American victory? _____

2. Name one battle that resulted in a Mexican victory? _____

3. What was the most southern battle? _____

4. What was the most northern battle? _____

5. In which two bodied of water did the U.S. Navy operate in the Mexican-American War?

_____

WESTWARD EXPANSION

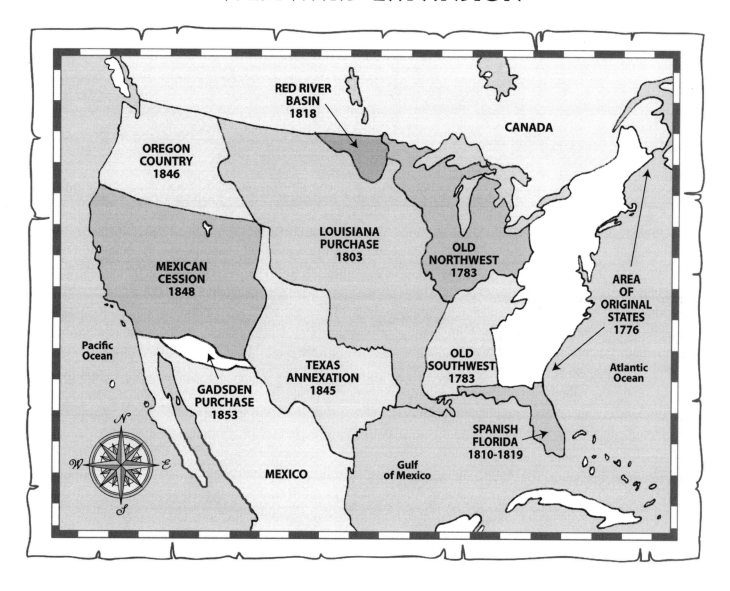

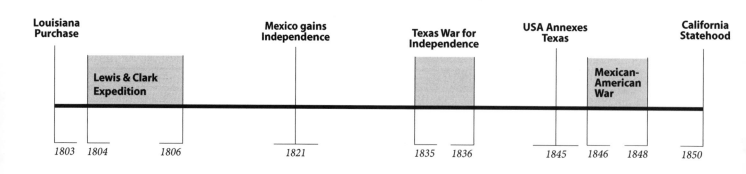

CHAPTER 49

THE CALIFORNIA GOLD RUSH AND THE OREGON TRAIL

California Gold Rush

Wagon Train

GRAMMAR
WHAT YOU NEED TO KNOW

1. **John Marshall:** While working at Sutter's Mill outside of Sacramento, California, John Marshall discovered a large nugget of gold in 1848. That started the California Gold Rush.

2. **'49ers:** In 1849, at least 100,000 men rushed into California searching for gold. These men were nicknamed "The 49ers."

3. **Cape Horn:** Cape Horn is at the southern tip of South America. Many 49ers came to California by sailing around Cape Horn.

4. **The Oregon Trail:** Beginning in Independence, Missouri and ending at the Pacific Ocean, the Oregon Trail was used by hundreds of thousands of Americans to move west.

5. **Oregon Treaty:** The Oregon Treaty (1846) established the Canadian-American border.

LOGIC
READING COMPREHENSION AND INFERENCE QUESTIONS

1. Based on the lesson, which name could be most appropriately given to those men who rushed into California in 1848 and 1849?

      a. Speedsters

      b. Gold Diggers

      c. Panners

      d. 48ers

Answer:

Which sentence(s) best supports the answer?

_____

_____

_____

2. Based on the lesson, you can infer that

      a. Some Californians became poor because of the gold rush.

      b. Most Californians became rich because of the gold rush.

      c. Some Californians became rich because of the gold rush.

      d. Most Californians became poor because of the gold rush.

Answer:

Which sentence(s) best supports the answer?

_____

_____

3. Based on the lesson, you can infer that the California Gold Rush

      a. helped make California the richest state because of gold.

      b. helped make California the poorest state because of gold.

      c. helped make California one of the richest farming states in the country.

      d. helped make Californians agriculturally sound.

Answer:

Which sentence(s) best supports the answer?

_____

_____

4. Based on the lesson, you can infer that the Oregon Trail

      a. brought only misery.

      b. brought only joy.

      c. wasn't that hard.

      d. was chosen as a path to success for people around the world.

Answer:

Which sentence(s) best supports the answer?

_____

_____

_____

5. Based on the lesson, you can infer that the Oregon Treaty

      a. ended conflict between Great Britain and the United States of America.

      b. brought Indians into the American society.

      c. emboldened many more Americans to go to Oregon.

      d. was signed after the Mexican-American War.

Answer:

Which sentence(s) best supports the answer?

_____

_____

RHETORIC
SHORT ANSWER QUESTIONS

Answer the following with a short essay (3-5 sentences):

1. What were the two easiest ways for New Yorkers to get to California in 1849?

_____

_____

_____

_____

2. In which way did most gold diggers find success in California?

_____

_____

_____

3. What were the three locations that travelers on the Oregon Trail went to?

_____

_____

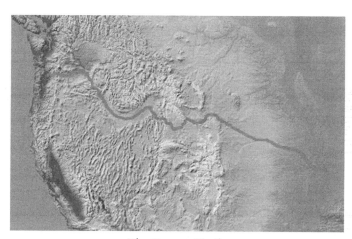

The Oregon Trail

MAP WORK
TEST YOUR KNOWLEDGE

Practice drawing and labeling the map, until you can do so by memory.

WESTWARD EXPANSION

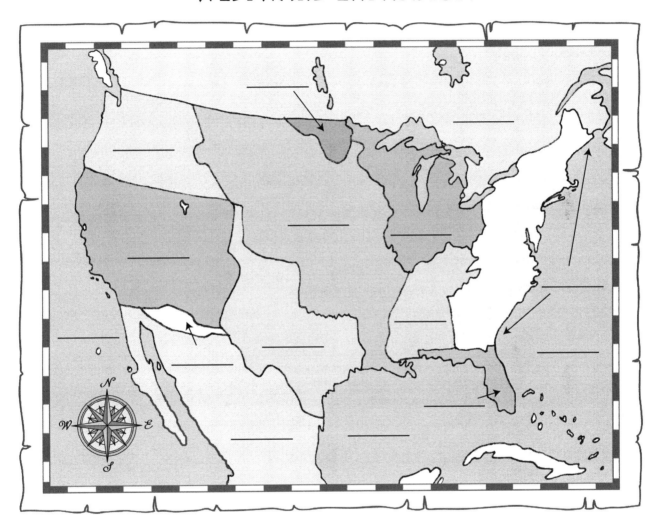

Answer these questions and test your knowledge.

1. Which purchase doubled the size of the U.S.A? _____

2. What word means when a country acquires land without war? _____

3. Which area on the map was the last to join the U.S.A? _____

4. What two oceans border the west and east of the U.S.A? _____

5. Under which President did the U.S.A. acquire Oregon Country and the Mexican Cession?

ACTIVITIES
UNIT 8

··· **RHETORIC** ·······································

WESTWARD EXPANSION · ACCOMPLISHMENT OR TRAGEDY?

QUESTION

In the years from 1820 to 1860 the United States grew to stretch "from sea to shining sea." The growth brought much accomplishment, but it also brought tragedy. Based on the evidence, did the 1800s expansion of the United States bring about accomplishment, tragedy, both, or neither? Was the expansion mainly an accomplishment or a tragedy?

Your teacher will assign you how many paragraphs to write. If writing a five-paragraph or more essay, research the following people and terms and attempt to use them in your writing. Notice that some of the following can be found in the preceding unit of *The Story of Liberty*.

Manifest Destiny	Mexican-American War	James K. Polk
Sequoyah	California Gold Rush	Oregon
representative democracy	Santa Anna	Northwest Ordinance
Laura Ingalls Wilder	Texas	Trail of Tears
Andrew Jackson		

PREWRITING ACTIVITIES FOR ESSAY #7

A. TAKING NOTES

Follow the structure below to write notes. Use a variety of sources.

MANIFEST DESTINY

What? _____

Who? _____

When? _____

Where? _____

Why? _____

Any other information? _____

Does this term show accomplishment, tragedy, both, or none? _____

Source: _____

MEXICAN-AMERICAN WAR

What? _____

Who? _____

When? _____

Where? _____

Why? _____

Does this term show accomplishment, tragedy, both, or none? _____

Source: _____

B. THE CAPITAL "T"

Write a large capital "T" on a separate piece of paper and title it as below. Fill in which terms and topics fit into one or both of these titles. Only list the terms and people.

ACCOMPLISHMENT(S)

1. _____
2. _____
3. _____
4. _____
5. _____
6. _____
7. _____
8. _____
9. _____
10. _____

TRAGEDY(IES)

1. _____
2. _____
3. _____
4. _____
5. _____
6. _____
7. _____
8. _____
9. _____
10. _____

C. THE MODIFIED CAPITAL "T"

You may want to list the term or person on the middle line of your paper instead. Write a few notes as to why or how this was part accomplishment and tragedy.

TERM: _____

ACCOMPLISHMENT(S)

_____

_____

TRAGEDY(IES)

_____

_____

C. DISCUSSION

When you share ideas with others, your ideas may be reinforced, rejected, or slightly changed. Listening to your classmates' ideas will help you form your own judgment. Likewise, if you are alone in a classroom or if you are learning with your teacher, it is important that you prepare all sides of an argument. Try to learn all sides of an argument and be prepared to defend all sides.

If you are in a classroom, each student should interview at least three classmates who do not sit next to one another. If you are in a classroom with one student, then the student needs to be able to argue both or many sides to one question. The answers to the following questions must be written down on a piece of paper.

1. WAS THE 1800s WESTWARD EXPANSION OF THE UNITED STATES OF AMERICA AN ACCOMPLISHMENT, A TRAGEDY, BOTH, OR NEITHER? WAS THE EXPANSION MAINLY AN ACCOMPLISHMENT OR A TRAGEDY?

2. WHY DO YOU THINK THIS?/ WHAT IS YOUR EVIDENCE?

Student 1:

Student 2:

Student 3:

REFLECTION

After you have written down all your classmates' responses, think about them and ask yourself the following questions. Write down your answers under your classmates' responses.

1. WHAT DO I THINK OF THESE CLASSMATES' ANSWERS?

2. WHICH ARE THE THREE BEST ANSWERS?

3. HAVE I CHANGED THE WAY I THINK? HOW?

You should now have a chance to present your ideas in a class discussion.

NOTES

COTTON PRODUCTION IN THE SOUTH
1790 - 1860

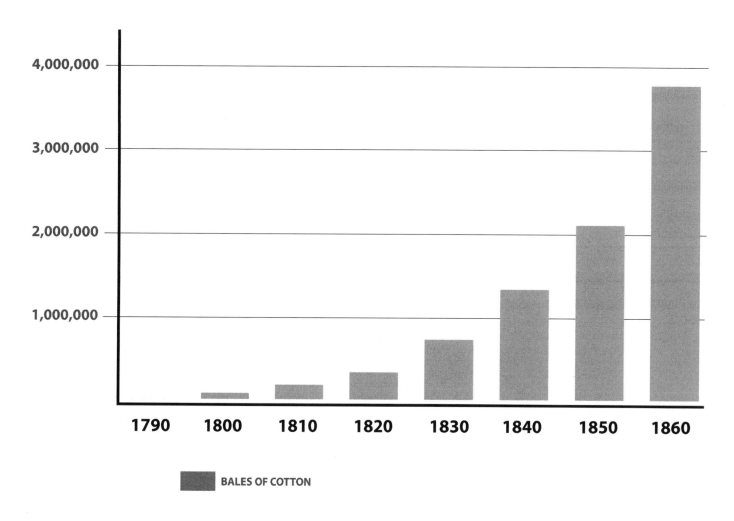

4,000,000

3,000,000

2,000,000

1,000,000

1790   1800   1810   1820   1830   1840   1850   1860

BALES OF COTTON

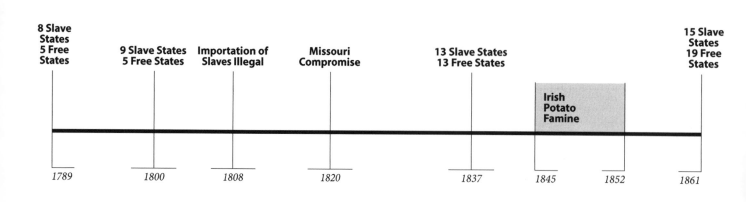

8 Slave
States
5 Free
States

9 Slave States
5 Free States

Importation of
Slaves Illegal

Missouri
Compromise

13 Slave States
13 Free States

Irish
Potato
Famine

15 Slave
States
19 Free
States

1789   1800   1808   1820   1837   1845   1852   1861

CHAPTER 50

THE SOUTH

Plantation

The South

GRAMMAR
WHAT YOU NEED TO KNOW

1. Gulf Coast and Coastal Plains: These areas were hot, humid, and flat. Plantations were located here.

2. Appalachian Mountains: The Appalachian Mountains run north and south from Canada to north-central Alabama.

3. Mississippi Delta: This area, from Memphis, Tennessee to Mississippi, provided rich cotton farmland.

4. Antebellum South: Antebellum South means Pre-war South.

5. Planters: Planters were 1% of the South's population and owned plantations.

6. Slaves: Slaves made up 33% of the South's Antebellum population.

7. George Fitzhugh: This American believed that nearly all should be slaves because it would free people from making decisions. The elite should make decisions.

8. Eli Whitney: Whitney invented the Cotton Gin, a machine that made it easier and more profitable to harvest cotton.

9. Cotton Kingdom: This became one nickname of the South because so much cotton was grown in the South.

10. Spirituals: Many slaves sang spirituals, songs inspired by the Gospel.

11. Population in the South in 1860: c. 5.8 million free people, c. 3.2 million slaves.

LOGIC
READING COMPREHENSION AND INFERENCE QUESTIONS

1. If you were a planter and owned a plantation, where in the South would you most likely have lived?

    a. Ozarks   b Appalachians

    c. Piedmont   d. Coastal Plains

Answer:

Which sentence(s) best supports the answer?

_____

_____

2. If you were a poor white farmer in the South, where would you most likely live?

    a. Massachusetts   b. Coastal Plains

    c. New York   d. Appalachians

Answer:

3. The largest group of people in the South was the

    a. slave   b. New Hampshire

    c. poor, white farmer   d. merchant

Answer

Which sentence(s) best supports the answer?

_____

_____

4. What kind of government existed in Antebellum South?

    a. Small   b. Large

    c. laissez-faire   d. Medium

Answer:

Which sentence(s) best supports the answer?

_____

_____

_____

5. Which of the following was not forbidden for slaves?

    a. Literacy   b. Gun Ownership
    c. Freedom of Movement   d. Religion

Answer:

Which sentence(s) best supports the answer?

_____

_____

RHETORIC
SHORT ANSWER QUESTIONS

Answer the following with a short essay (3-5 sentences):

1. Why did slavery in the South require a large government?

Answer:

_____

_____

_____

_____

_____

2. Explain two of the arguments pro-slavery Southerners used to explain how slavery is good.

Answer:

_____

_____

_____

_____

_____

_____

3. Did slavery help or hurt the Southern economy?

Answer:

_____

_____

_____

_____

_____

_____

_____

Cotton Production in the South 1790 - 1860

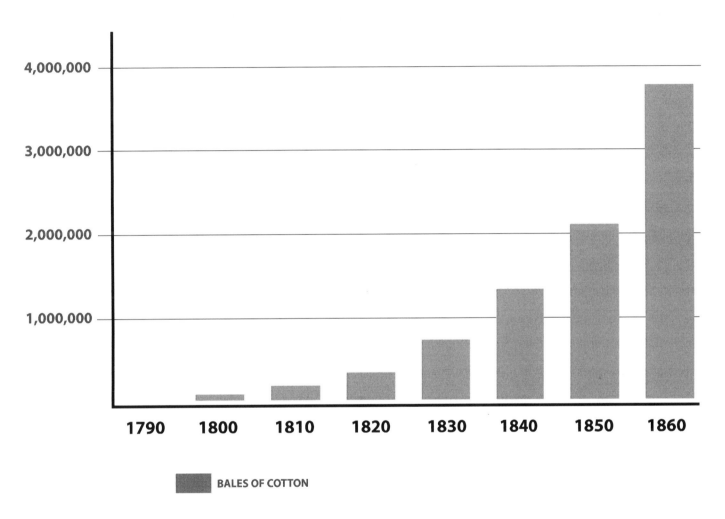

BALES OF COTTON

Answer these questions and test your map knowledge.

1. **About how many bales of cotton were produced in 1850?** _____

2. **About how many bales of cotton were produced in 1830?** _____

3. **About how many bales of cotton were produced in 1860?** _____

4. **Which 20 years saw the production of cotton go from under 2,000,000 to almost 4,000,000?**

_____

5. **How would you describe the production of cotton in America from 1790 to 1860?** _____

_____

THE NORTH & SOUTH, 1860

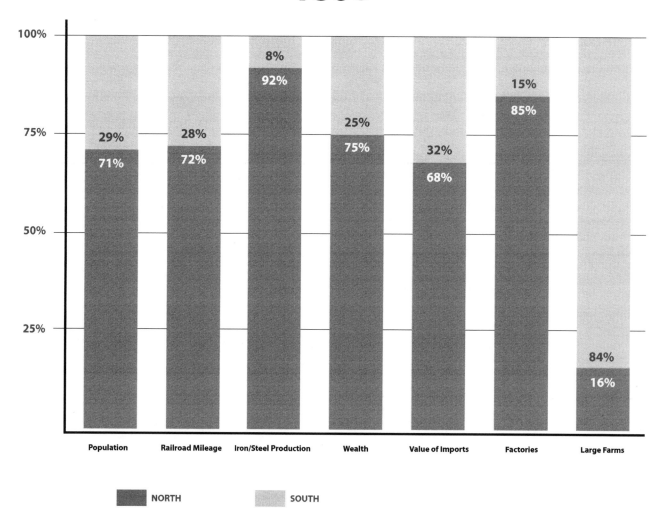

| | Population | Railroad Mileage | Iron/Steel Production | Wealth | Value of Imports | Factories | Large Farms |

NORTH ■   SOUTH □

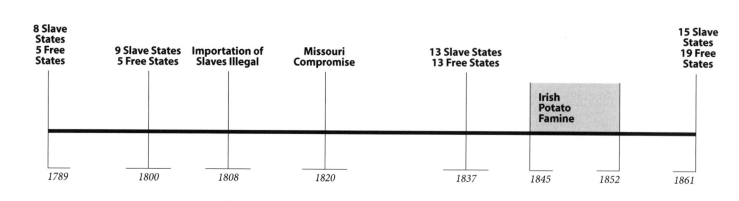

8 Slave States 5 Free States

9 Slave States 5 Free States

Importation of Slaves Illegal

Missouri Compromise

13 Slave States 13 Free States

Irish Potato Famine

15 Slave States 19 Free States

1789   *1800*   *1808*   *1820*   *1837*   *1845*   *1852*   *1861*

CHAPTER 51

THE NORTH

The North

GRAMMAR
WHAT YOU NEED TO KNOW

1. Northeast: The Northeast has warm, humid summers and cold, snowy winters. It is hilly and rocky.

2. The Midwest: The Midwest has ample forests, the Great Lakes, and thousands of lakes and rivers.

3. The Erie Canal: The Erie Canal connected the Great Lakes to the Hudson River and eventually to New York City.

4. Capitalism in the North: In the North, capitalism enabled individuals to improve their lives and create the world's strongest economy.

5. Industrial Revolution in the North: In the North, many moved from farms to the cities for better jobs and more opportunities.

6. Robert Fulton: Fulton established one of the first steamboat transportation systems.

7. 1860 Population in the North: 22 million.

8. Cornelius Vanderbilt: Vanderbilt used technology and business skills to make ocean travel less expensive and faster.

9. Five Points Neighborhood: Five Points Neighborhood was a dangerous area in New York City.

10. Mills: Mills were small factories powered by running water. Many were located in the North.

LOGIC
READING COMPREHENSION AND INFERENCE QUESTIONS

1. Which area was best suited for dairy farms?

a. New England   b. Midwest

c. Appalachians   d. Ohio River

Answer:

Which sentence(s) best supports this answer?

_____

_____

2. What is not one reason for the successful economy of the North?

a. Capitalism   b. Immigration

c. Slavery   d. Limited Government

Answer:

Which sentence(s) best supports this answer?

_____

_____

_____

3. Which of the following was one area where the South led the North?

a. Number of People   b. Number of Plantations

c. Imports   d. Industrial Products

Answer:

4. If you were a policeman in 1860, which area would have caused you the most trouble during your workday?

a. Cockroach Row

b. Hell-Cat Maggie

c. The Daybreak Boys

d. The Dead Rabbits

Answer:

Which sentence(s) best supports this answer?

_____

_____

5. In the mid-1800s, if you needed to get to California and you lived in New York City, which of the following would be best able to help you?

a. Hell-Cat Maggie

b. Robert Fulton

c. The Dead Rabbits

d. Cornelius Vanderbilt

Answer:

Which sentence(s) best supports this answer?

_____

_____

_____

RHETORIC
SHORT ANSWER QUESTIONS

Answer the following with a short essay (3-5 sentences):

1. How did making slavery illegal affect the North?

_____

_____

_____

_____

_____

_____

_____

2. Explain how the Industrial Revolution allowed women to have more economic opportunities.

Answer:

_____

_____

_____

_____

_____

_____

_____

_____

_____

_____

3. Why did most of the immigrants in the 1800s go to the North and not to the South?

Answer:

_____

_____

_____

_____

_____

_____

_____

THE NORTH & SOUTH, 1860

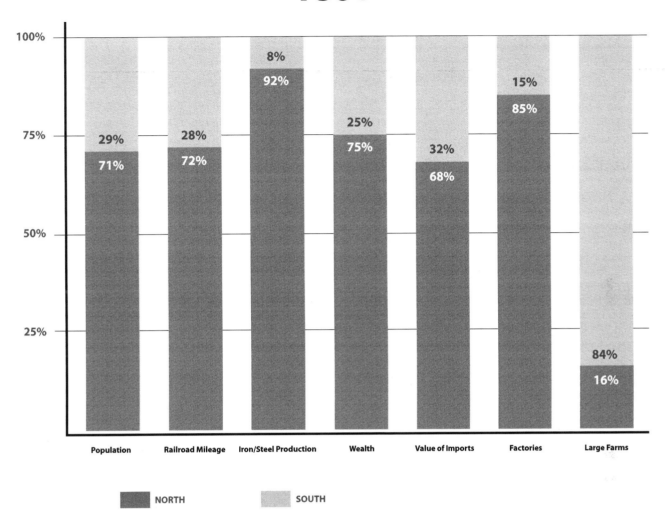

Answer these questions and test your knowledge.

1. Which part of the country led in the percentage of farming? _____

2. Which part of the country led in areas of industry? _____

3. Which industrial section did the North lead the South by the greatest percentage? _____

_____

4. Which industrial section did the North lead the South by the least percentage? _____

5. If you were an investor in large farms, where might most of your investments be? _____

TRAILS WEST

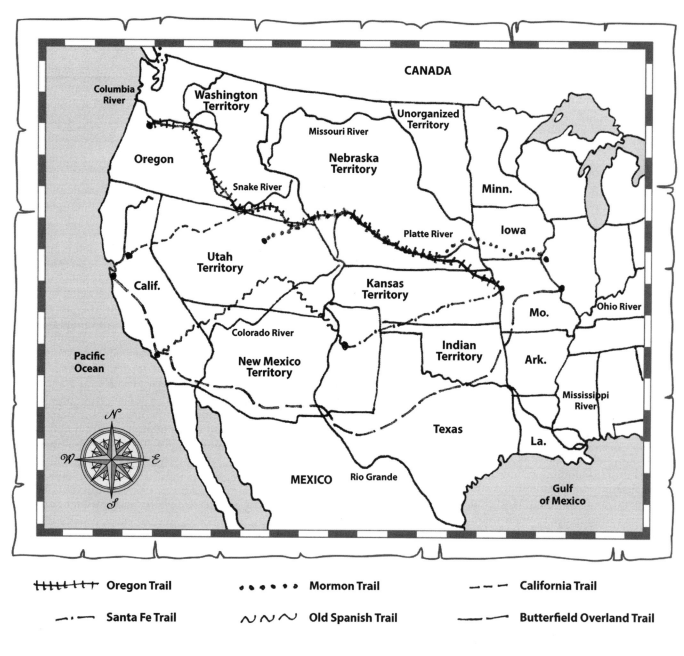

HHHHHH **Oregon Trail**   •••••• **Mormon Trail**   — — — **California Trail**

—··— **Santa Fe Trail**   ᘒᘒᘒ **Old Spanish Trail**   ——— **Butterfield Overland Trail**

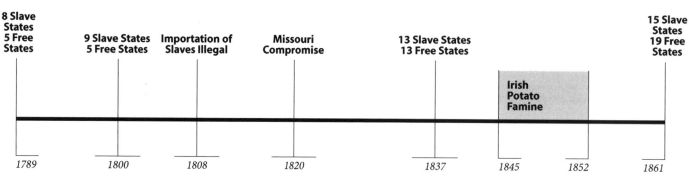

CHAPTER 52

LIFE IN THE WEST

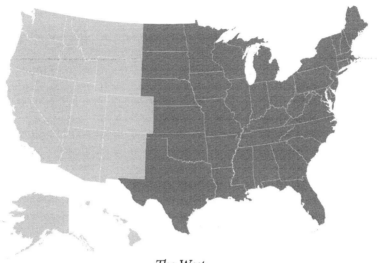

The West

GRAMMAR
WHAT YOU NEED TO KNOW

1. Frontier: The frontier was the area just beyond American civilization. In the 1800s, the frontier continually moved west.

2. Fur Trappers: Fur trappers hunted for animals with fur, such as beaver, fox, deer, and bear.

3. Jedediah Strong Smith: Smith was a mountain man who mapped much of the West.

4. Davy Crockett: Crockett was a frontiersman, volunteer soldier, state representative, and soldier who was killed at the Battle of the Alamo.

5. Conestoga Wagon: Pioneer families went by Conestoga Wagon to the west.

6. Mountain Men: Mountain men explored, mapped, and hunted animal pelts in the west before pioneer families moved west.

7. Comanche Indians: Comanche Indians are a Native American people who occupied the southern Plains.

LOGIC
READING COMPREHENSION AND INFERENCE QUESTIONS

1. Based on the lesson, you can infer that the West

      a. stayed the same.

      b. was different depending on the time period.

      c. was very similar to the North.

      d. was open to slavery.

Answer:

Which sentence(s) best supports this answer?

_____

_____

2. Based on the lesson, the frontier

      a. was safe.

      b. was a convenient place to start a home.

      c. was easy.

      d. had many challenges.

Answer:

Which sentence(s) best supports this answer?

_____

_____

3. Based on the lesson, you can infer that Thomas Jefferson

      a. overestimated the rate of inhabiting the West.

      b. underestimated how fast the West would be inhabited.

      c. misunderstood the colonization of America.

      d. understood the colonization of America.

Answer:

Which sentence(s) best supports this answer?

_____

_____

4. Place the following in chronological order:

        a. Davy Crockett is killed.

        b. 1783

        c. Lewis and Clark Expedition

        d. Jedediah Smith is killed

Answer:

5. Based on the lesson, you can infer that Davy Crockett

        a. always supported Andrew Jackson

        b. always supported Martin Van Buren

        c. was against Tennesseans

        d. was talented in many areas

Answer:

Which sentence(s) best supports this answer?

_____

_____

_____

RHETORIC
SHORT ANSWER QUESTIONS

Answer the following with a short essay (3-5 sentences):

1. Based on this lesson, and your knowledge of the Trail of Tears, would you describe Davy Crockett as a friend, or an enemy, of the Indians?

_____

_____

_____

_____

_____

_____

2. Which group of people were most responsible for the expansion of American culture in the 1800s?

Answer:

_____

_____

_____

_____

_____

3. Explain how the life of a mountain man, or the life of living in the frontier, could be dangerous.

Answer:

_____

_____

_____

_____

_____

TRAILS WEST

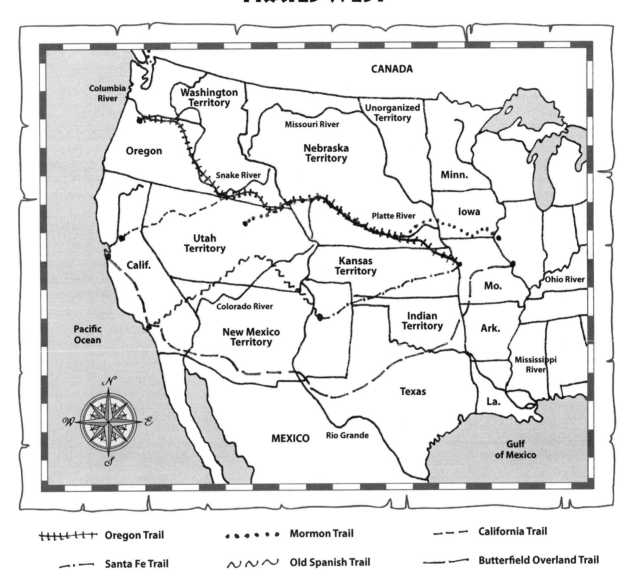

⊢⊢⊢⊢⊣⊣⊢	Oregon Trail	• • • • • •	Mormon Trail	– – –	California Trail
–·–·–	Santa Fe Trail	∿∿∿∿	Old Spanish Trail	––––––	Butterfield Overland Trail

Answer these questions and test your knowledge.

1. Name two trails that led west? _____

2. In which state did the Oregon Trail begin? _____

3. In which state did the Santa Fe Trail begin? _____

4. In which state did the Old Spanish Trail end in the West? _____

5. In which state did the Overland Butterfield Overland Trail end in the west? ____

COMPOSITION OF IMMIGRATION, 1840-1860

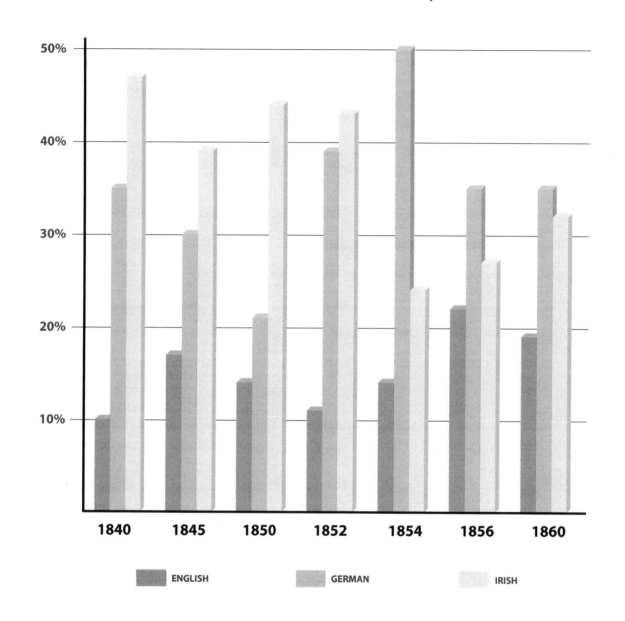

50%

40%

30%

20%

10%

| 1840 | 1845 | 1850 | 1852 | 1854 | 1856 | 1860 |

ENGLISH   GERMAN   IRISH

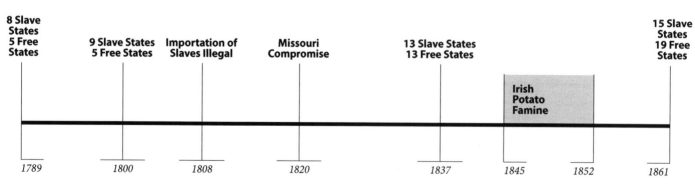

8 Slave States 5 Free States

9 Slave States 5 Free States

Importation of Slaves Illegal

Missouri Compromise

13 Slave States 13 Free States

15 Slave States 19 Free States

Irish Potato Famine

1789   *1800*   *1808*   *1820*   *1837*   *1845*   *1852*   *1861*

CHAPTER 53

IMMIGRATION

Immigration

GRAMMAR
WHAT YOU NEED TO KNOW

1. Capitalism: In capitalism, individuals have great freedom how to make and spend money and how to buy property. Many immigrants moved to America because of capitalism.

2. Slaves: In 1860, somewhere between 3.2 million and 3.8 million slaves were in America.

3. E Pluribus Unum: One of America's mottos, E Pluribus Unum, means, "From many, we are one." This means that many nationalities come to America, but in the new land, everyone becomes one people, Americans.

4. Immigrants: An immigrant is someone who permanently leaves his home to live in another land, and usually, eventually becomes a citizen.

5. Potato Famine: In Ireland in the 1840s, potatoes were diseased, and the English did not send food or help to Ireland. Over 1 million died and 2 million moved to America.

6. Tammany Hall: Tammany Hall was a Democratic political machine in New York City. Corrupt Democratic politicians paid off people to win their votes.

7. Revolutions of 1848: The European revolutions of 1848 drove many Germans and central Europeans to move to America.

LOGIC
READING COMPREHENSION AND INFERENCE QUESTIONS

1. What is not one reason many immigrants moved to the North and West of the U.S.A. during the 1800s?

      a. slavery

      b. capitalism

      c. weather

      d. limited government

Answer:

2. Based on the lesson, why did so many immigrants choose the United States of America over other countries in the 1800s?

      a. racism

      b. sexism

      c. feminism

      d. equality under the law

Answer:

Which sentence(s) best supports this answer?

_____

_____

_____

3. Based on the lesson, you can infer that outside of the U.S.A. in the 1800s, many

      a. individuals were treated unfairly and had few rights.

      b. individuals had the same rights as Americans.

      c. people had problems with their family.

      d. people were naturally good.

Answer:

Which sentence(s) best supports this answer?

_____

_____

_____

4. Based on the lesson, you can infer that the Irish

        a. hated America because they were discriminated against.

        b. loved America because they were discriminated against.

        c. chose America because of problems in Ireland.

        d. chose America because Irish were Protestant Christians.

Answer:

Which sentence(s) best supports this answer?

_____

_____

_____

5. Based on the lesson, you can infer that German immigrants to America

        a. hated all monarchs.

        b. wanted to ban alcohol in America.

        c. had knowledge in manufacturing.

        d. were just like the Irish.

Answer:

Which sentence(s) best supports this answer?

_____

_____

_____

RHETORIC
SHORT ANSWER QUESTIONS

Answer the following with a short essay (3-5 sentences):

1. Compare and contrast the reasons the Irish and the Germans immigrated to America in the 1800s.

_____

_____

_____

_____

_____

_____

_____

_____

_____

_____

2. Why did the Irish face more discrimination in America than the Germans?

_____

_____

_____

_____

3. Why did most immigrants to America move to the North and West but not to the South?

_____

_____

_____

_____

_____

_____

COMPOSITION OF IMMIGRATION, 1840 - 1860

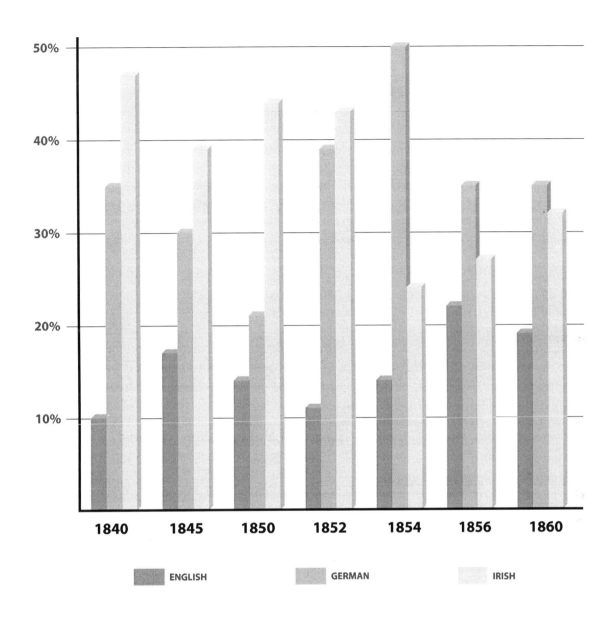

ENGLISH   GERMAN   IRISH

Answer these questions and test your knowledge.

1. In which year was the largest percentage of immigrants German? _____

2. In which year was the largest percentage of immigrants Irish? _____

3. In which year was the least percentage of immigrants English? _____

4. In which three years was there a higher percentage of German immigrants than Irish

   immigrants? _____

5. In which years were there more Irish than German immigrants?

   _____

ACTIVITIES
UNIT 9

RHETORIC
OPEN-ENDED ESSAY

BACKGROUND

In many ways, the United States of America at its founding in 1776 was a union of 13 unique countries. Soldiers under General Washington refused to give an oath to the country, because they felt they were fighting for their state. Americans in the North did not necessarily agree with Americans in the South on key issues. Over the next century, these differences between the North and South became greater. Slavery was outlawed in the North, but it was a way of life in the South. In addition, a new section of the country emerged: the West. However, in many ways, the West was more similar to the North than to the South.

THE ASSIGNMENT

Compare and contrast the Antebellum North with the Antebellum South.

RESEARCH ACTIVITIES

A. COMPARE AND CONTRAST

Follow the structure below to write notes. Use a variety of sources.

NORTH		**SOUTH**
Contrasts	Common	Contrasts

_____

_____

_____

_____

_____

_____

_____

B. GEOGRAPHY

1. Describe the geography of the North.

_____

_____

_____

_____

_____

_____

_____

_____

_____

_____

_____

_____

2. Describe the geography and climate of the South.

_____

_____

_____

_____

_____

_____

_____

_____

_____

_____

_____

_____

_____

C. THE UNDERGROUND RAILROAD

Describe the Underground Railroad

_____
_____
_____
_____
_____
_____
_____
_____
_____
_____

D. DISCUSSION

1. What were the greatest similarities between the North and the South?

_____
_____
_____
_____
_____

2. What were the greatest differences between the North and the South?

_____
_____
_____
_____
_____

NOTES

THE COMPROMISE OF 1850

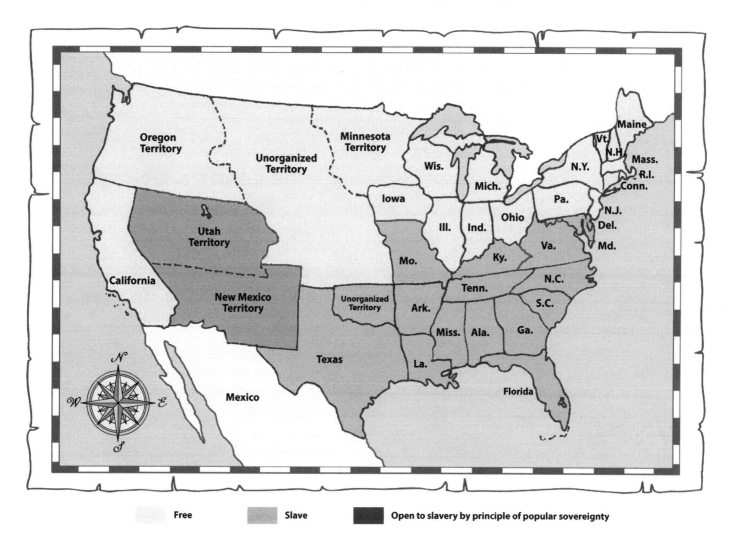

Free Slave Open to slavery by principle of popular sovereignty

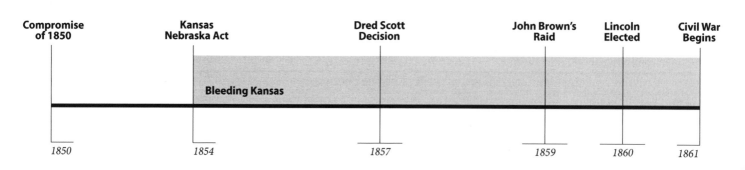

Compromise of 1850	Kansas Nebraska Act	Dred Scott Decision	John Brown's Raid	Lincoln Elected	Civil War Begins

Bleeding Kansas

1850   1854   1857   1859   1860   1861

CHAPTER 54

POLITICAL INSTABILITY AND THE END OF WESTWARD EXPANSION

Zachary Taylor

Millard Fillmore

GRAMMAR
WHAT YOU NEED TO KNOW

1. **Popular Sovereignty:** Popular sovereignty meant that each state would decide to be a free or a slave state.

2. **Martin Van Buren:** Martin Van Buren founded the Democratic Party and the Free Soil Party.

3. **The Compromise of 1850:**
    a. California entered as a free state.
    b. Citizens of the future Utah and New Mexico would decide by popular sovereignty if they would be free or slave.
    c. Texas western border was agreed upon.
    d. The slave trade was eliminated in Washington, D.C.
    e. A stronger Fugitive Slave Law forced Northerners to capture and return runaway slaves.

1. From 1837 to 1860, what word best describes how Americans thought about their Presidents?

      a. love

      b. hatred

      c. ambivalent

      d. determined

Answer:

Which sentence(s) best supports this answer?

_____

_____

_____

2. Based on the lesson, you can infer that the result of the Mexican-American War

      a. resolved the slavery problem for the South.

      b. caused more problems for the United States of America.

      c. caused the slavery problem for the North and South.

      d. had nothing to do with slavery.

Answer:

Which sentence(s) best supports this answer?

_____

_____

_____

3. Which of the following terms best describes the position of Northern politicians who were personally against slavery but argued they did not want to make laws against slavery.

      a. fascism

      b. permissive

      c. judgmental

      d. insane

Answer:

4. What was the number one reason for the rapid growth of the California population?

        a. a precious metal

        b. oil

        c. trees

        d. Mexican-American War

Answer:

Which sentence(s) best supports this answer?

_____

_____

_____

5. Place the following in chronological order:

        a. California admitted to the Union

        b. Beginning of the Mexican-American War

        c. America wins the Mexican Cession

        d. The Missouri Compromise

Answer:

RHETORIC
SHORT ANSWER QUESTIONS

Answer the following with a short essay (3-5 sentences):

1. What do historians Michael Allen and Larry Schweikart mean when they write, "not to call evil, evil is to call it good?"

Answer:

_____

_____

_____

_____

_____

2. How did the success of America in the Mexican-American War also cause its problems?

Answer:

_____

_____

_____

_____

_____

_____

3. How does the author of *The Story of Liberty* tear down the philosophy of "live and let live."

Answer:

_____

_____

_____

MAP WORK
TEST YOUR KNOWLEDGE

THE COMPROMISE OF 1850

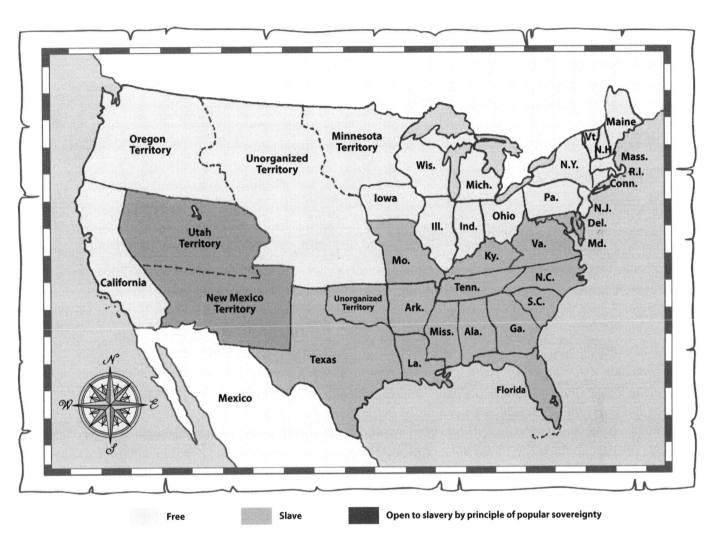

Free   Slave   Open to slavery by principle of popular sovereignty

Answer these questions and test your map knowledge.

1. Was California a free or a slave state? _____

2. What was The New Mexico territory? _____

3. Was Iowa a free or a slave state? _____

4. In 1850, how many slave states were there? _____

5. In 1850, how many free states were there? _____

KANSAS - NEBRASKA ACT, 1854

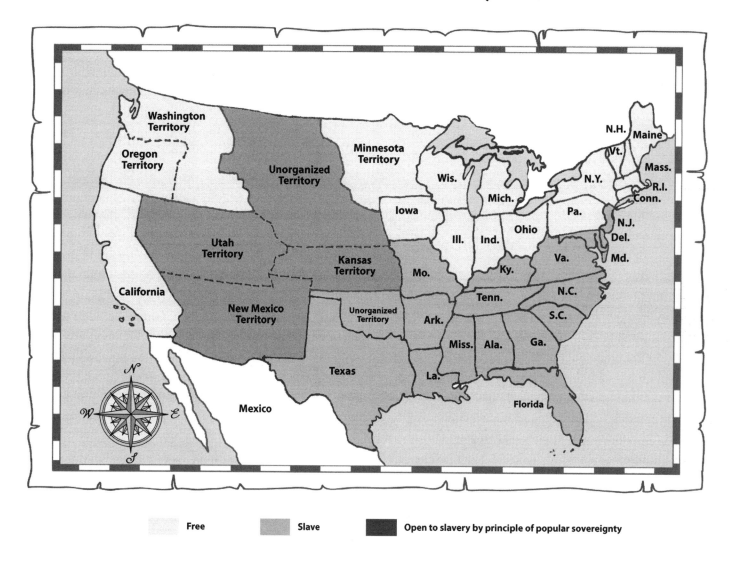

Free   Slave   Open to slavery by principle of popular sovereignty

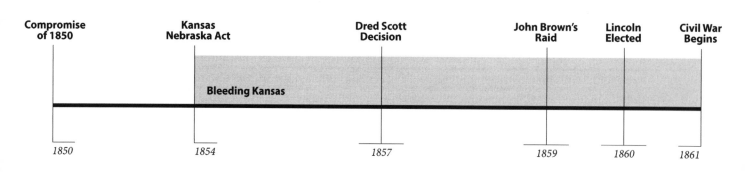

| Compromise of 1850 | Kansas Nebraska Act | Dred Scott Decision | John Brown's Raid | Lincoln Elected | Civil War Begins |

Bleeding Kansas

1850   1854   1857   1859   1860   1861

CHAPTER 55

THE DECADE PRECEDING THE CIVIL WAR

Franklin Pierce

James Buchanan

GRAMMAR
WHAT YOU NEED TO KNOW

1. Harriet Beecher Stowe: Stowe wrote *Uncle Tom's Cabin*, a novel against slavery.

2. Kansas-Nebraska Act: The Kansas-Nebraska Act (1854) stated that Kansans and Nebraskans would vote if their states would become free or slave.

3. Bleeding Kansas: Before Kansans voted if the state would be free or slave, anti-slavery forces fought against pro-slavery forces.

4. John Brown: John Brown was a radical abolitionist who led men to kill pro-slavery individuals.

5. Senator Charles Sumner: South Carolina Democrat Congressman Preston Brooks beat Republican Massachusetts Senator Charles Sumner because Sumner gave an impassioned anti-slavery speech.

6. Dred Scott decision: The Supreme Court decided that slaves were slaves not only in Southern states, but throughout all the territories, as well.

7. Harper's Ferry: In 1859, John Brown led a small army and broke into a federal arsenal and tried to lead an assault of slaves against their masters in the South. Brown was caught and executed.

LOGIC
READING COMPREHENSION AND INFERENCE QUESTIONS

1. *Uncle Tom's Cabin*, **by Harriet Beecher Stowe...**

      a. was the main reason for the Civil War.

      b. was a true depiction of slavery.

      c. was completely false and not based on anything in reality.

      d. influenced many to believe in the harshness of slavery.

Answer:

Which sentence(s) best supports this answer?

_____

_____

2. Based on the lesson, you can infer that Stephen Douglas' legislation regarding Kansas and Nebraska

      a. was a complete success.

      b. was somewhat successful.

      c. was somewhat a failure.

      d. was a cause for bloodshed.

Answer:

Which sentence(s) best supports this answer?

_____

_____

3. In the 1850s, at least one U.S. Congressmen

      a. was murdered by abolitionists.

      b. encouraged violence.

      c. was African-American.

      d. was murdered by pro-slavery groups.

Answer:

Which sentence(s) best supports the answer?

_____

_____

4. In the beating of Senator Charles Sumner over his anti-slavery speech in Congress, which of the following can you infer?

      a. The pro-slavery Republican beat the anti-slavery Democrat.

      b. The anti-slavery Republican beat the pro-slavery Democrat.

      c. The pro-slavery Democrat beat the anti-slavery Republican.

      d. The anti-slavery Democrat beat the pro-slavery Republican.

Answer:

Which sentence(s) best supports this answer?

_____

_____

_____

_____

_____

_____

_____

5. Which of the following can you infer about politics in the 1850s?

      a. Democrats favored popular sovereignty.

      b. Republicans didn't take a stand on slavery.

      c. The American Party was strongly against slavery.

      d. Irish Catholics didn't like to vote.

Answer:

Which sentence(s) best supports this answer?

_____

_____

_____

_____

RHETORIC
SHORT ANSWER QUESTIONS

1. How does the Dred Scott decision go against American ideals as expressed in the Declaration of Independence?

Answer:

_____

_____

_____

_____

2. How did John Brown's raid on Harper's Ferry influence how Southerners thought of Northerners?

Answer:

_____

_____

_____

3. What is one reason that popular sovereignty did not work as a solution to the slavery issue?

Answer:

_____

_____

_____

_____

_____

_____

_____

_____

_____

MAP WORK
TEST YOUR KNOWLEDGE

KANSAS - NEBRASKA ACT, 1854

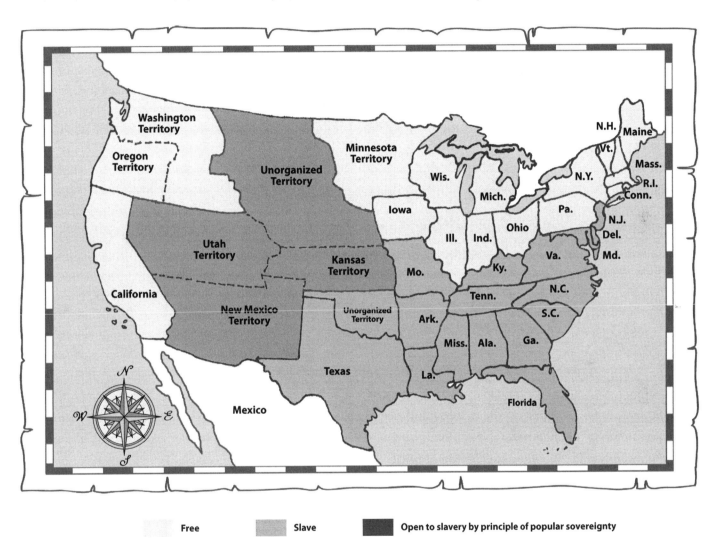

Free   Slave   Open to slavery by principle of popular sovereignty

Answer these questions and test your map knowledge.

1. **Was the Unorganized Territory near Canada free, slave, or open to slavery?** _____

2. **Which two territories were open to slavery?** _____

3. **Which territories were free?** _____

4. **Was the Unorganized Territory near Arkansas free, slave, or open to slavery?** _____

5. **In 1854, how many states were free and how many states were slave?** <u>16 free, 15 slave</u>

ABRAHAM LINCOLN, 1809 - 1847

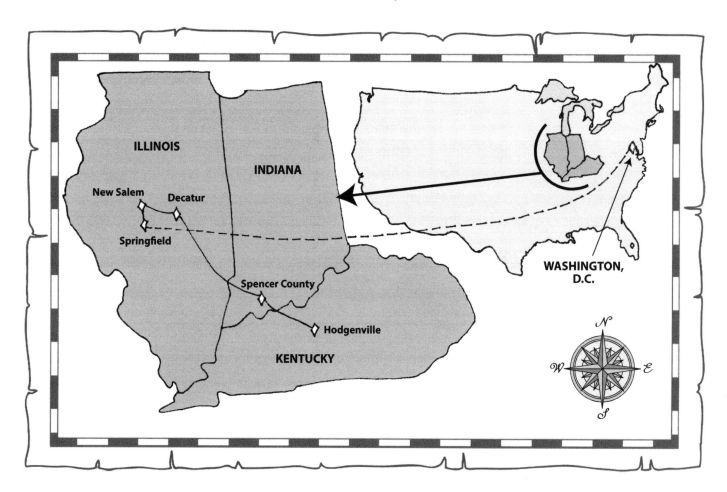

Hodgenville, Kentucky	Born February 12, 1809
Spencer County, Indiana	1816 - 1830 Family lived here
Decatur, Illinois	1830 - 1831 Moved with Family
New Salem, Illinois	1831 - 1837 Worked as a clerk, storeowner, postmaster, surveyor, legislator
Springfield, Illinois	1837 Lawyer and Legislator
Washington D.C.	1847 Lawyer and Legislator

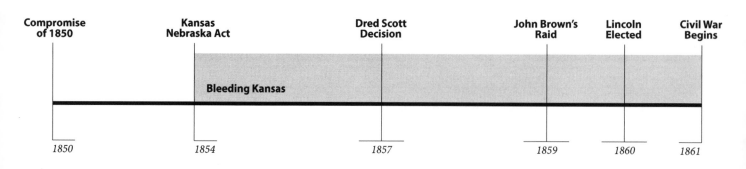

UNIT 10: THE SLAVERY CRISIS BECOMES VIOLENT, 1848-1860

CHAPTER 56

ABRAHAM LINCOLN

Abraham Lincoln

RAMMAR
WHAT YOU NEED TO KNOW

1. Lincoln's opinion on the morality of slavery: Lincoln thought that slavery was a moral evil.

2. Lincoln's opinion on slavery in the U.S.A. before the election: Lincoln didn't want slavery to expand.

3. Abraham Lincoln's Youth: Abraham Lincoln was the 16th President, he lived 1809 – 1865, he was born in Kentucky, moved to Indiana at the age of 9, and moved to Illinois at the age of 21.

4. Lincoln's profession: Lincoln was a lawyer.

5. Lincoln's religious views: Lincoln became a Christian but was not in a particular denomination.

6. Lincoln's family: Lincoln married Mary Todd, had four sons, three who died before turning 19.

7. Lincoln-Douglas Debates: Campaigning for Illinois Senator, Lincoln became well known as an anti-slavery candidate with morals during the Lincoln-Douglas Debates.

LOGIC
READING COMPREHENSION AND INFERENCE QUESTIONS

1. Based on the lesson, you can infer

    a. Illinois voters liked Stephen Douglas better than Abraham Lincoln as a political leader in 1858.

    b. Illinois voters liked Abraham Lincoln better than Stephen Douglas as a political leader in 1858.

    c. Illinois voters liked Stephen Douglas better than Abraham Lincoln as a political candidate in 1860.

    d. Illinois voters liked Abraham Lincoln better than Stephen Douglas as a political leader in 1860.

Answer:

Which sentence(s) best supports this answer?

_____

_____

_____

2. Based on the lesson, Lincoln believed the institution of slavery

    a. was a necessary evil.

    b. was against God.

    c. should be immediately abolished.

    d. should be left alone as it's not his business.

Answer:

Which sentence(s) best supports this answer?

_____

_____

3. Based on the lesson, what was not one reason Mary Todd married Abraham Lincoln?

    a. He was a politician.

    b. He was thinking about being a President.

    c. He was handsome.

    d. He was tall and strong.

Answer:

Which sentence(s) best supports this answer?

_____

_____

_____

4. Based on the lesson, it appears Lincoln had a conversion experience

      a. during the election.

      b. during the war.

      c. after the war.

      d. when he moved to Indiana.

Answer:

Which sentence(s) best supports this answer?

_____

_____

_____

5. Based on the lesson, Lincoln's education

      a. was mainly in the classroom.

      b. was primarily because of his mother.

      c. was primarily from books.

      d. was attained during the Civil War.

Answer:

Which sentence(s) best supports this answer?

_____

_____

_____

_____

RHETORIC
SHORT ANSWER QUESTIONS

Answer the following with a short essay (3-5 sentences):

1. Why does the author of _The Story of Liberty_ claim that Lincoln was "the most hated and despised president of all time, yet he is one of America's greatest presidents?"

_____

_____

_____

_____

2. What are examples in Lincoln's life that he was a man of courage?

Answer:

_____

_____

_____

_____

_____

_____

3. How was Lincoln's life filled with tragedy?

Answer:

_____

_____

_____

Abraham Lincoln, 1809 - 1847

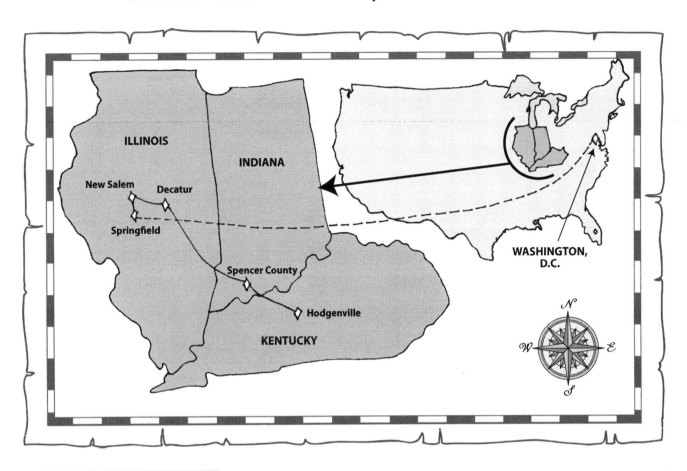

Hodgenville, Kentucky	Born February 12, 1809
Spencer County, Indiana	1816 - 1830 Family lived here
Decatur, Illinois	1830 - 1831 Moved with Family
New Salem, Illinois	1831 - 1837 Worked as a clerk, storeowner, postmaster, surveyor, legislator
Springfield, Illinois	1837 Lawyer and Legislator
Washington D.C.	1847 Lawyer and Legislator

Answer these questions and test your knowledge.

1. Where was Abraham Lincoln born? _____

2. From about the age of 7 to 21, where did Abraham Lincoln live? _____

3. Where did Lincoln work as a storeowner? _____

4. Before moving to Washington, D.C., about how many places did Lincoln live? _____

5. What was Lincoln's last city that he lived in? _____

# ACTIVITIES
UNIT 10

RHETORIC
OPEN-ENDED ESSAY

THE CIVIL WAR, CAUSES
BACKGROUND

From the beginning of the United States up to the Civil War different sections of the country seemed to form separate entities. Historians usually refer to these sections as the North, the South, and the West. Some of these differences would cause our country's most costly war in human suffering, the Civil War, 1861–1865. Other people and events also led to the Civil War.

QUESTION

What were the two most important causes of the Civil War?

THESE ARE TERMS YOU SHOULD BE FAMILIAR WITH TO ANSWER THE QUESTION:

19th century immigration
slavery
the Underground Railroad
Compromise of 1820, 1850
Bleeding Kansas
Lincoln-Douglas Debates

industrialization
states' rights
Abraham Lincoln
agriculture
Kansas-Nebraska Act

the Cotton Kingdom
Texas
abolitionism
Dred Scott Decision

A. TAKING NOTES

Follow the structure below to write notes. You may need to research into previous units to find your answers.

IMMIGRATION

What? _____

Who? _____

When? _____

Where? _____

Why? _____

Any other information? _____

_____

What role, if any, did this have in creating differences between sections of the United States?

_____

INDUSTRIALIZATION

What? _____

Who? _____

When? _____

Where? _____

Why? _____

Any other information? _____

_____

What role, if any, did this have in creating differences between sections of the United States?

_____

B. CAUSE AND EFFECT

CAUSE AND EFFECT is a term that means one event made another event happen. For example, if you push against the pedals of your bicycle, the bicycle moves. In this example, the push against the pedals is the cause and the bicycle moving is the effect.

CAUSE ------------------------------→ **EFFECT**
push against pedals--------------→ bicycle moves

In history, cause and effect usually relates events and people. The relationship is trickier to understand than the above example with the bicycle. Sometimes it is difficult to see causes and effects in history. Here are two examples from American history with which most historians would agree.

CAUSE ------------------------------→ **EFFECT**
Japan attacks Pearl Harbor--------→ the United States enters World War II
the U.S. drops atomic bombs on Japan -------→ Japan surrenders

CAUSE	EFFECT	RANK

C. DISCUSSION

When you share ideas with others, your ideas may be reinforced, rejected, or slightly changed. Listening to your classmates' ideas will help you form your own judgment. Likewise, if you are alone in a classroom or if you are learning with your teacher, it is important that you prepare all sides of an argument. Try to learn all sides of an argument and be prepared to defend all sides.

If you are in a classroom, each student should interview at least three classmates who do not sit next to one another. If you are in a classroom with one student, the one student should be able to discuss all possible answers to the question.

1. WHAT WERE THE TWO GREATEST CAUSES OF THE CIVIL WAR?

2. WHY DO YOU THINK THIS?/ WHAT IS YOUR EVIDENCE?

Student 1: _____

_____

Student 2: _____

_____

Student 3: _____

_____

REFLECTION

After you have written down all your classmates' responses, think about them and ask yourself the following questions. Write down your answers under your classmates' responses.

1. WHAT DO I THINK OF THESE CLASSMATES' ANSWERS? _____

_____

2. WHICH ARE THE THREE BEST ANSWERS? _____

_____

3. HAVE I CHANGED THE WAY I THINK? HOW? _____

_____

You should now have a chance to present your ideas in a class discussion. If somebody says something with which you disagree, speak up! In your discussion, you may find out he is actually right and you are wrong. All possible viewpoints should be stated and defended out loud. Test your ideas in class.

THE ELECTION OF 1860

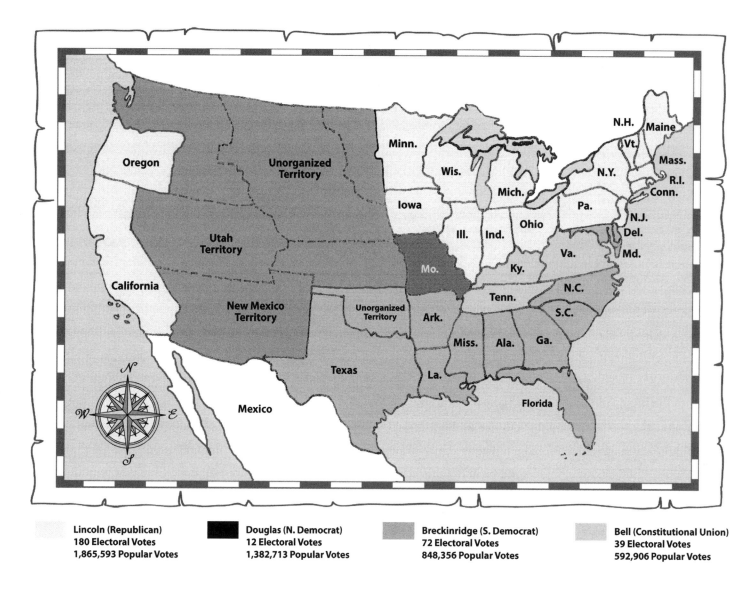

Lincoln (Republican) 180 Electoral Votes 1,865,593 Popular Votes	Douglas (N. Democrat) 12 Electoral Votes 1,382,713 Popular Votes	Breckinridge (S. Democrat) 72 Electoral Votes 848,356 Popular Votes	Bell (Constitutional Union) 39 Electoral Votes 592,906 Popular Votes

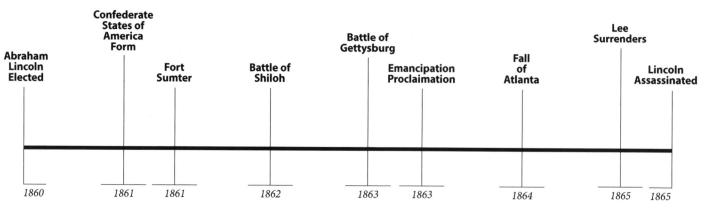

UNIT 11: THE CIVIL WAR

CHAPTER 57

THE ELECTION OF 1860

WHAT YOU NEED TO KNOW

1. The Election of 1860:

    a. Southern Democrat John C. Breckenridge: Breckinridge favored a national law enforcing slavery.

    b. Northern Democrat Stephen Douglas: Douglas wanted popular sovereignty as the solution to the slavery issue.

    c. Constitutional Unionist John Bell: Bell favored slavery, but did not demand a national law enforcing slavery.

    d. Republican Abraham Lincoln: Lincoln viewed slavery as immoral and was against its expansion.

    e. Results: Lincoln won the electoral vote, and Republicans won a majority in the Senate and House of Representatives.

LOGIC
READING COMPREHENSION AND INFERENCE QUESTIONS

1. Based on the lesson, what can you infer about Americans in 1860?

       a. Most Americans were pro-slavery.

       b. Most Americans were extremely racist.

       c. Most Americans were against slavery.

       d. We don't know what most Americans thought.

Answer:

Which sentence(s) best supports your answer?

_____

_____

_____

2. What percentage of the 1860 vote did the two most-anti-slavery candidates win?

       a. 19

       b. 69%

       c. 33%

       d. 14

Answer:

Which sentence(s) best supports your answer?

_____

_____

_____

RHETORIC
SHORT ANSWER QUESTIONS

Answer the following with a short essay (3-5 sentences):

1. In 1860, were the majority of Americans pro-slavery or anti-slavery?

Answer:

_____

_____

_____

_____

_____

THE ELECTION OF 1860

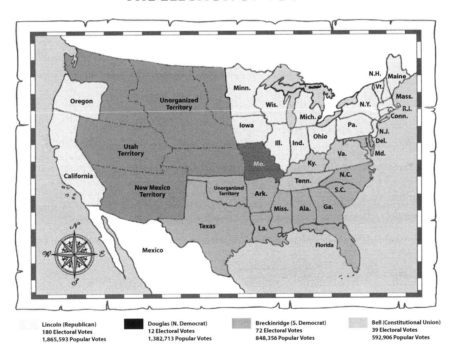

Lincoln (Republican)	Douglas (N. Democrat)	Breckinridge (S. Democrat)	Bell (Constitutional Union)
180 Electoral Votes	12 Electoral Votes	72 Electoral Votes	39 Electoral Votes
1,865,593 Popular Votes	1,382,713 Popular Votes	848,356 Popular Votes	592,906 Popular Votes

Answer these questions and test your knowledge.

1. What percent of the popular vote did Lincoln win? _____

2. What percent of the electoral vote did Lincoln win? _____

3. Which two candidates were against the expansion of slavery? _____

4. What percent of the popular vote did Lincoln and Douglas win? _____

5. Breckenridge supported the expansion of slavery. What percent of the popular vote did he win?

THE CIVIL WAR, 1861-1865

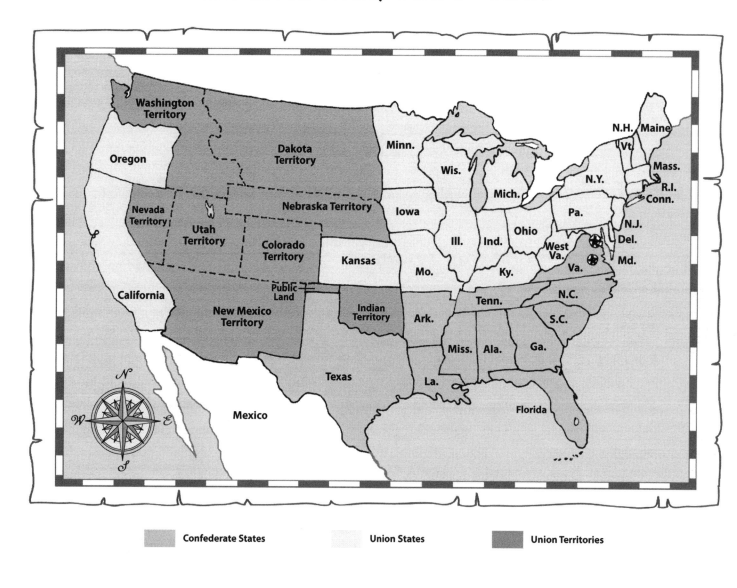

Confederate States   Union States   Union Territories

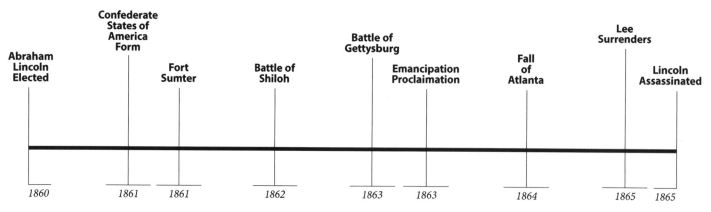

Abraham Lincoln Elected — 1860

Confederate States of America Form — 1861

Fort Sumter — 1861

Battle of Shiloh — 1862

Battle of Gettysburg — 1863

Emancipation Proclaimation — 1863

Fall of Atlanta — 1864

Lee Surrenders — 1865

Lincoln Assassinated — 1865

CHAPTER 58

SECESSION AND THE CONFEDERATE STATES OF AMERICA

Jefferson Davis

GRAMMAR
WHAT YOU NEED TO KNOW

1. Secession: Secession means to leave the United States of America. The Southern states seceded after Lincoln's election.

2. The Confederate States of America: Eleven Southern states seceded from the United States of America and formed The Confederate States of America (C.S.A.).

3. Slavery and Race: Each Southern state's secession document declared that secession was necessary to protect slavery.

4. Jefferson Davis: Davis was the President of the C.S.A.

5. States' Rights: States' Rights refers to the idea that each state has rights over the federal government.

LOGIC
READING COMPREHENSION AND INFERENCE QUESTIONS

1. Based on the lesson, Southern states

       a. had more rights in the C.S.A. than in the U.S.A.

       b. had less rights in the U.S.A. than in the C.S.A.

       c. had more rights in the U.S.A. than in the C.S.A.

       d. had no rights.

Answer:

Which sentence(s) best supports this answer?

_____

_____

2. Which is one name Southerners did not call Northerners after secession?

       a. Scalawag

       b. jailbird

       c. busy bodies

       d. meddlers

Answer:

3. Which product of the South did Southerners believe would allow them to secede and control their future?

       a. Slavery

       b. Tobacco

       c. Indigo

       d. Cotton

Answer:

Which sentence(s) best supports this answer?

_____

_____

RHETORIC
SHORT ANSWER QUESTIONS

Answer the following with a short essay (3-5 sentences):

1. Were all Southerners in favor of secession?

_____

_____

_____

_____

_____

_____

_____

_____

THE CIVIL WAR, 1861-1865

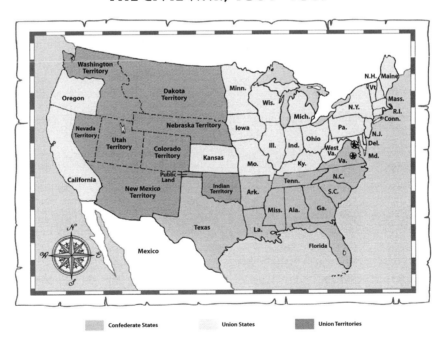

Confederate States   Union States   Union Territories

Answer these questions and test your map knowledge.

1. How many states were in the Confederate States of America? _____

2. How many states remained in the Union? _____

3. How many border states stayed in the Union? _____

4. What was the most western Union state? _____

5. What was the most western Confederate state? _____

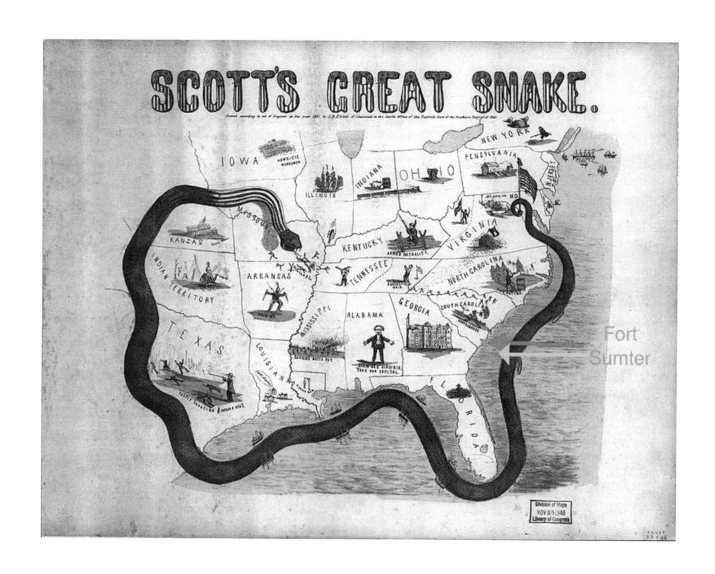

Fort
Sumter

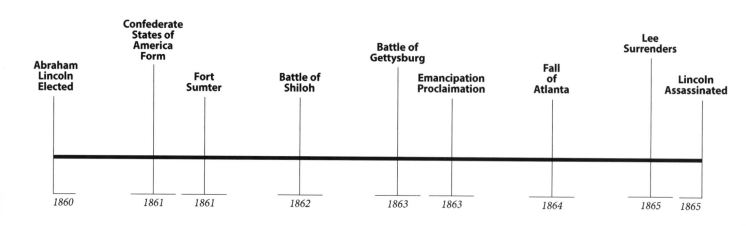

CHAPTER 59

FORT SUMTER AND THE WAR ON PAPER

Fort Sumter

GRAMMAR
WHAT YOU NEED TO KNOW

1. Fort Sumter: On April 12th and April 13th, the South attacked the North on the island of Fort Sumter, South Carolina. This was the first battle of the Civil War.

2. Rebellion: Lincoln called the conflict the "rebellion" and never the "civil war."

3. 1860 Population: In 1860, there were 22 million Northerners and 9 million Southerners. 3.2 million of Southerners were slaves.

4. Gatling Gun: The Gatling Gun is a rapid-fire weapon, the forerunner of the machine gun.

5. Robert E. Lee: Lee was the commander of the Army of Northern Virginia, and the South's main military leader.

6. Anaconda Plan: The North's initial strategy was to control the Mississippi River, blockade the South on the Gulf Coast and Southern coast, and to squeeze the South. This was called the Anaconda Plan.

7. Hard War: The North modified its original war strategy to execute a two-front war and to wage war on much of the Southern population.

8. King Cotton: The South believed that Great Britain and France needed Southern cotton so much that they would assist the South in defeating the U.S.A.

9. Attack and Die: The South lost many more soldiers in the war than the North.

10. Commander-in-Chief: President Lincoln was an able Commander-in-Chief for the North and Jefferson Davis was an incompetent one for the South.

11. Ulysses S. Grant: Grant eventually become the General-in-Chief of the North's armies, after Lincoln had hired and demoted a number of generals who had failed at the position.

LOGIC
READING COMPREHENSION AND INFERENCE QUESTIONS

1. Based on the lesson, you can infer that

      a. The North wanted to defend states' rights.

      b. Lincoln's election triggered the South's secession.

      c. The South wanted to defend the federal government.

      d. President Buchanan adequately addressed the slavery issue.

Answer:

Which sentence(s) best supports the answer?

_____

_____

2. Based on the lesson, Lincoln can be described as

      a. decisive

      b. indecisive

      c. wishy washy

      d. arrogant

Answer:

Which sentence(s) best supports the answer?

_____

_____

_____

_____

3. Based on the lesson,

      a. the South held more tangible advantages than the North.

      b. the North held more intangible advantages than the South.

      c. the South held less intangible advantages than the North.

      d. the South held more intangible advantages than the North.

Answer:

Which sentence(s) best supports the answer?

_____

_____

_____

4. Based on the lesson, Lincoln

        a. wanted to abolish slavery immediately.

        b. wanted to abolish slavery over time.

        c. wanted to defend slavery.

        d. wanted to expand slavery.

Answer:

Which sentence(s) best supports the answer?

_____

_____

_____

5. In the Confederate States of America,

        a. all citizens had to pay taxes for slavery, even if they did not own slaves.

        b. only citizens who owned slaves had to pay taxes for slaves.

        c. all slaves had to pay taxes for slavery.

        d. all Northerners had to pay taxes for slavery.

Answer:

Which sentence(s) best supports the answer?

_____

_____

RHETORIC
SHORT ANSWER QUESTIONS

Answer the following with a short essay (3-5 sentences):

1. Did the "Attack and Die" philosophy of the South help or hinder it in the Civil War?

_____

_____

_____

_____

_____

_____

2. Based on the population, soldiers, volunteers, and other tangibles, which side held the advantage in the Civil War?

Answer:

_____

_____

_____

_____

_____

3. Which society, Antebellum North or South, was more capitalistic? Explain your answer.

Answer:

_____

_____

_____

_____

_____

_____

MAP WORK
TEST YOUR KNOWLEDGE

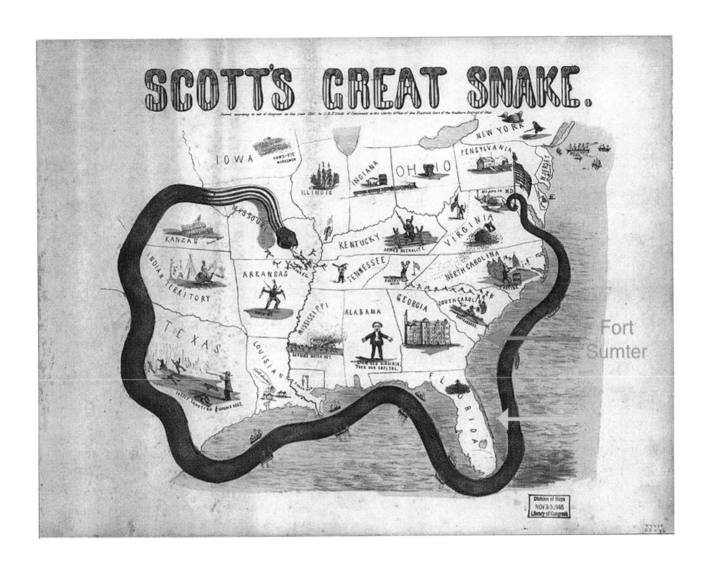

Answer these questions and test your knowledge.

1. After which animal was the Union war plan named? _____

2. What was the Union military supposed to do, based on this plan? _____

3. What was the Union War Plan called? _____

4. Which state was Fort Sumter a part of? _____

5. Which large river divided the Southern states? _____

Battle Hymn of the Republic

Mine eyes have seen the glory of the coming of the Lord
He is trampling out the vintage where the grapes of wrath are stored,
He has loosed the fateful lightning of His terrible swift sword
His truth is marching on.
Chorus:
Glory! Glory! Hallelujah!
Glory! Glory! Hallelujah!
Glory! Glory! Hallelujah!
His truth is marching on.
I have seen Him in the watch-fires of a hundred circling camps
They have builded Him an altar in the evening dews and damps
I can read His righteous sentence by the dim and flaring lamps
His day is marching on.
Chorus
I have read a fiery gospel writ in burnish`d rows of steel,
"As ye deal with my contemnors, so with you my grace shall deal;"
Let the Hero, born of woman, crush the serpent with his heel
Since God is marching on.
Chorus
He has sounded from the trumpet that shall never call retreat
He is sifting out the hearts of men before His judgment-seat
Oh, be swift, my soul, to answer Him! Be jubilant, my feet!
Our God is marching on.
Chorus
In the beauty of the lilies Christ was born across the sea,
With a glory in His bosom that transfigures you and me:
As He died to make men holy, let us die to make men free,
While God is marching on.
Julia Ward Howe, 1861

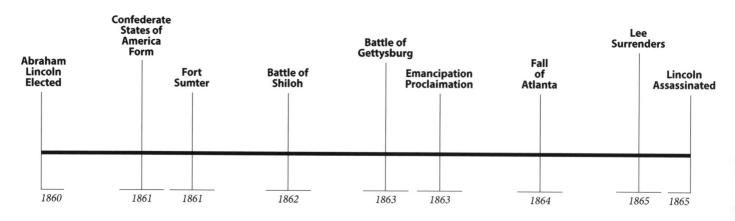

Abraham Lincoln Elected	Confederate States of America Form	Fort Sumter	Battle of Shiloh	Battle of Gettysburg	Emancipation Proclaimation	Fall of Atlanta	Lee Surrenders	Lincoln Assassinated
1860	1861	1861	1862	1863	1863	1864	1865	1865

UNIT 11: THE CIVIL WAR

CHAPTER 60

BULL RUN AND THE BEGINNING OF THE WAR

The Civil War

Monitor versus Merrimack

GRAMMAR
WHAT YOU NEED TO KNOW

1. **Battle of Bull Run:** On July 16, 1861, the South won.

2. **Richmond, Virginia:** Richmond was the capital of the C.S.A.

3. **Washington, D.C:** Washington, D.C. is the capital of the U.S.A.

4. **Stonewall Jackson:** Thomas "Stonewall" Jackson was a Confederate commander in the Civil War.

5. **Blockade:** The North blockaded the South during the war. This means that Northern ships did not allow Southern ships to leave or enter the C.S.A.

6. *Monitor* **v.** *Merrimack:* The *Monitor* and the *Merrimack* were two iron-plated ships that faced each other in battle. In the future, all modern navies had ships with metal sides.

LOGIC
READING COMPREHENSION AND INFERENCE QUESTIONS

1. Based on the lesson, you can infer that many Americans thought

      a. the war would be entertaining.

      b. the North could never win the war.

      c. the South could only tie.

      d. the Battle of Bull Run was necessary.

Answer:

Which sentence(s) best supports the answer?

_____

_____

2. Place the following in chronological order:

      a. *Monitor* v. *Merrimack*

      b. The Battle of Bull Run

      c. Fort Sumter is attacked

      d. Lincoln is elected President

Answer:

3. In the first part of the war, where did the North achieve success?

      a. The North

      b. The South

      c. The West

      d. The Atlantic Ocean

Answer:

Which sentence(s) best supports the answer?

_____

_____

_____

4. Based on the lesson, what is one word that can be used to describe General McDowell?

     a. patient

     b. serene

     c. hasty

     d. ignorant

Answer:

Which sentence(s) best supports the answer?

_____

_____

5. What may have helped the North a great deal?

     a. the loss at the Battle of Bull Run

     b. General Pope

     c. General McDowell

     d. General Burnside

Answer:

Which sentence(s) best supports the answer?

_____

_____

RHETORIC
SHORT ANSWER QUESTIONS

Answer the following with a short essay (3-5 sentences):

1. During the first part of the war, what was most successful for the North?

_____

_____

_____

_____

_____

2. In what ways was General McClellan unsuccessful as General-in-Chief?

Answer:

_____

_____

_____

_____

_____

3. What was "strange" or "interesting" that the South chose Richmond as their capital?

Answer:

_____

_____

_____

_____

Battle Hymn of the Republic

Mine eyes have seen the glory of the coming of the Lord
He is trampling out the vintage where the grapes of wrath are stored,
He has loosed the fateful lightning of His terrible swift sword
His truth is marching on.
Chorus:
Glory! Glory! Hallelujah!
Glory! Glory! Hallelujah!
Glory! Glory! Hallelujah!
His truth is marching on.
I have seen Him in the watch-fires of a hundred circling camps
They have builded Him an altar in the evening dews and damps
I can read His righteous sentence by the dim and flaring lamps
His day is marching on.
Chorus
I have read a fiery gospel writ in burnish`d rows of steel,
"As ye deal with my contemnors, so with you my grace shall deal;"
Let the Hero, born of woman, crush the serpent with his heel
Since God is marching on.
Chorus
He has sounded from the trumpet that shall never call retreat
He is sifting out the hearts of men before His judgment-seat
Oh, be swift, my soul, to answer Him! Be jubilant, my feet!
Our God is marching on.
Chorus
In the beauty of the lilies Christ was born across the sea,
With a glory in His bosom that transfigures you and me:
As He died to make men holy, let us die to make men free,
While God is marching on.
Julia Ward Howe, 1861

Answer these questions and test your knowledge.

1. Based on this popular Union song, many Americans held which religious belief? _____

2. What does "let us die to make men free" mean? _____

_____

3. Based on this song, did Northern soldiers pray to ask God for victory? _____

4. Who is this line about, "Let the Hero, born of woman, crush the serpent with his heel?"

_____

5. Did the author believe God was on the side of the North or the South? _____

NATIONAL DEBT, 1858-1865

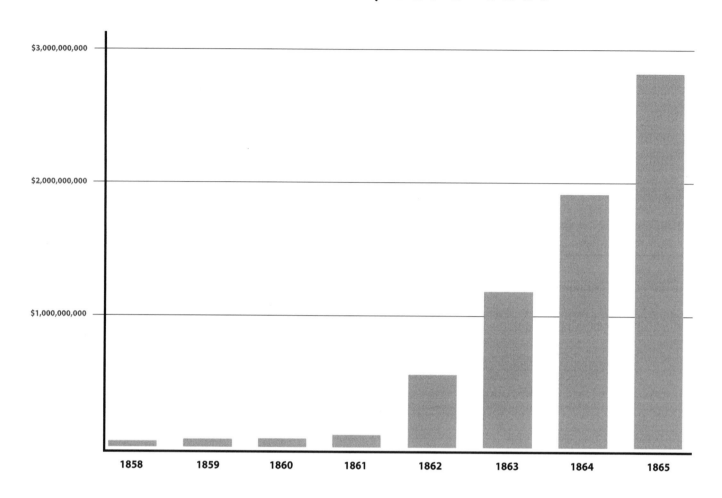

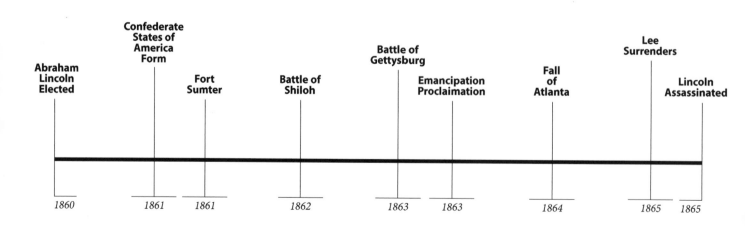

CHAPTER 61

GROWTH OF GOVERNMENT

The Union Army, 1865

GRAMMAR
WHAT YOU NEED TO KNOW

1. GNP: Gross National Product is the sum of everything the country produces.

2. Pork-Barrel Legislation: Pork-barrel legislation means laws that Congressmen pass to get reelected.

3. National Banking Acts of 1863 and 1864: These two laws monopolized money, taxed income, sold bonds, instituted paper money, created a national banking system, and grew the federal government.

LOGIC
READING COMPREHENSION AND INFERENCE QUESTIONS

1. Based on the lesson, the federal government of the North

      a. took over power from the states

      b. allowed states more power than the South

      c. was in great debt because of the war

      d. was good

Answer:

Which sentence(s) best supports this answer?

2. Based on the lesson, many laws were passed in the North

      a. that hurt the North

      b. that lost the war

      c. to get Northerners reelected

      d. all the time

Answer:

Which sentence(s) best supports this answer?

3. During the Civil War, economically, economically, the U.S. government carried out policies that did what, in relation to the free market?

      a. weakened

      b. helped

      c. built

      d. completely destroyed

Answer:

Which sentence(s) best supports this answer?

RHETORIC
SHORT ANSWER QUESTIONS

Answer the following with a short essay (3-5 sentences):

1. Why did Lincoln encourage the growth of government during the Civil War?

_____

_____

_____

_____

NATIONAL DEBT, 1858-1865

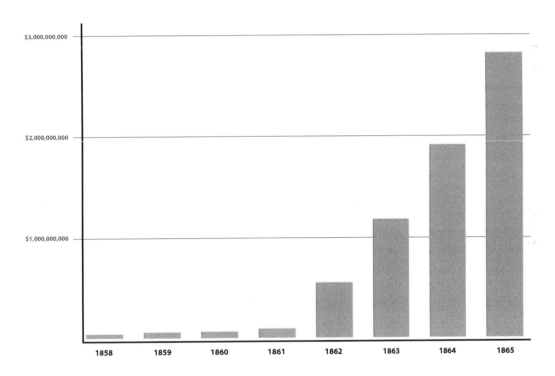

Answer these questions and test your knowledge.

From 1858 – 1860, was the National Debt much less or much more than 1,000,000,000? _____

2. From 1861 to 1862, did the National Debt more triple? _____

3. During the war, from 1861-1865, describe the National Debt. _____

4. In 1865, was the National Debt closer to 2 or 3 billion? _____

5. Based on this chart, what is one thing the Federal government did to fund the war?

Major Civil War Battle Casualties

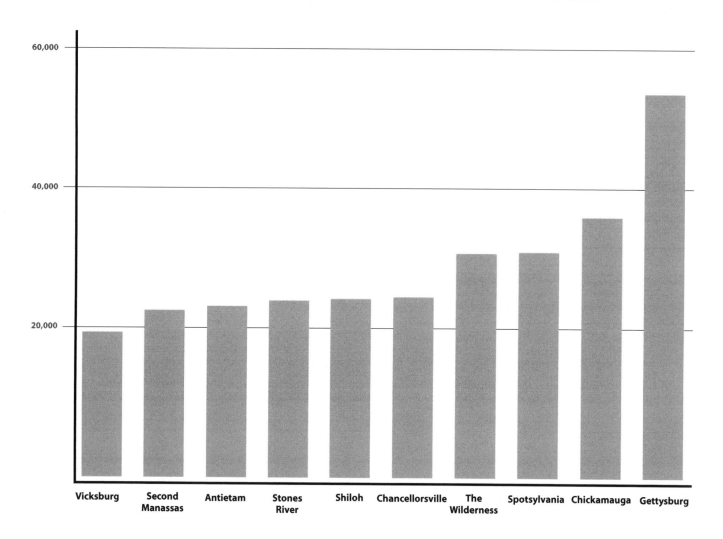

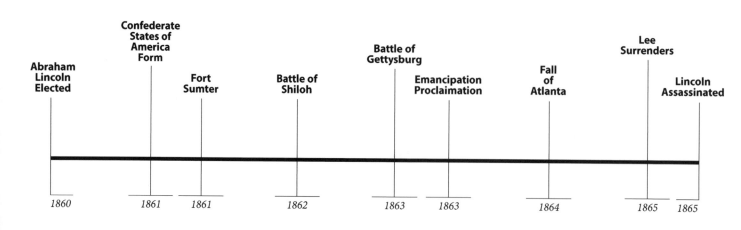

CHAPTER 62

THE EMANCIPATION PROCLAMATION

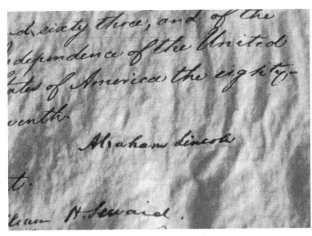

The Emancipation Proclamation

Abraham Lincoln

RAMMAR
WHAT YOU NEED TO KNOW

1. Emancipation: Emancipation means the freeing of someone from slavery.

2. Emancipation Proclamation: On January 1, 1863, the Emancipation Proclamation took effect. It freed the slaves in the rebelling states.

3. Battle of Antietam: At the Battle of Antietam in Maryland, General McClellan defeated General Lee, and over 24,000 were killed or wounded. After the Battle, Lincoln issued the Emancipation Proclamation.

4. Sabotage: Sabotage means when someone destroys something. After the Emancipation Proclamation, slaves committed more acts of sabotage.

LOGIC
READING COMPREHENSION AND INFERENCE QUESTIONS

1. Lincoln's Emancipation Proclamation

      a. freed all the slaves in the U.S.A.

      b. freed the slaves in the Northern states of the U.S.A.

      c. freed the slaves in the Southern states of the U.S.A.

      d. freed the slaves in the rebelling states of the U.S.A.

Answer:

Which sentence(s) best supports the answer?

2. What effect did the Emancipation Proclamation not have?

      a. Slaves sabotaged Southern war efforts.

      b. Black Americans fought in the Civil War.

      c. Great Britain and France did not want to support the South.

      d. Abolitionists hated Lincoln.

Answer:

3. Place the following in chronological order:

      a. Emancipation Proclamation takes effect

      b. McClellan discovers Lee's battle plans

      c. 24,000 are wounded or die at the Battle of Antietam

      d. Lee invaded Maryland

Answer:

RHETORIC
SHORT ANSWER QUESTIONS

Answer the following with a short essay (3-5 sentences):

1. Describe how Lincoln explained the paradox of private property and slavery.

_____

_____

_____

_____

2. How did Abraham Lincoln's Emancipation Proclamation make the Civil War a war to end slavery?

_____

_____

_____

_____

_____

_____

_____

_____

MAJOR CIVIL WAR BATTLE CASUALTIES

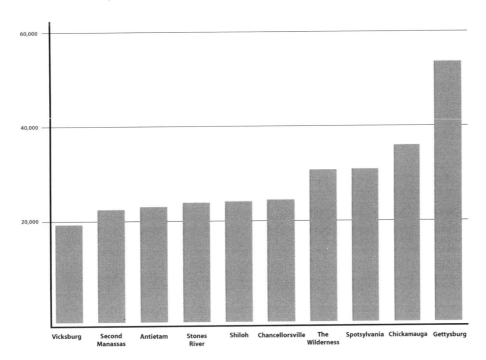

Answer these questions and test your knowledge.

1. Which battle was the bloodiest of the Civil War? _____

2. Which battles of the Civil War had around 30,000 casualties? _____

_____

3. Name two battles that had a little over 20,000 casualties. _____

4. At least how many battles had over 20,000 casualties? _____

5. Name one battle that had a little under 20,000 casualties. _____

CASUALTIES OF THE CIVIL WAR

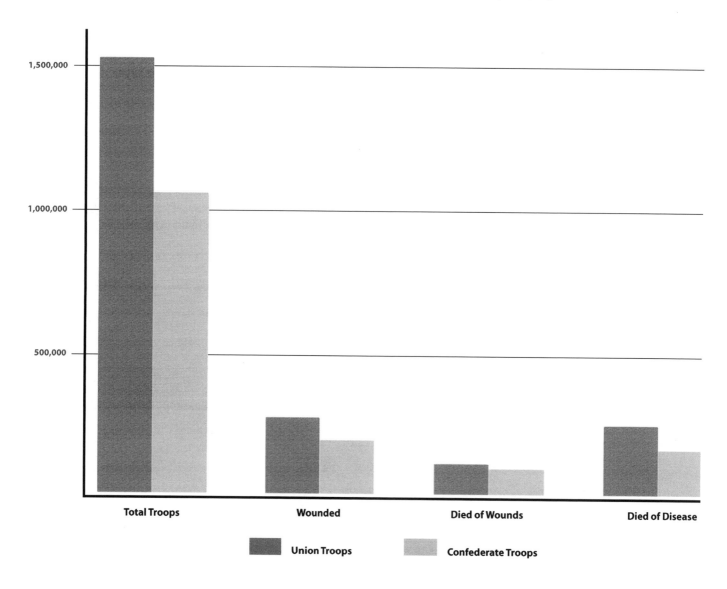

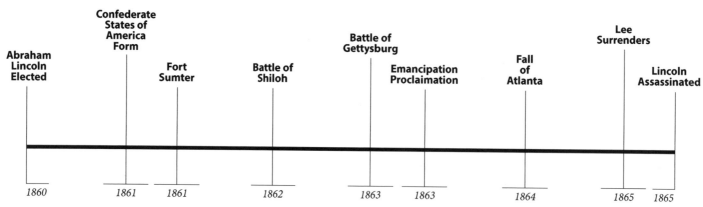

CHAPTER 63

HARD WAR

Civil War Dead

WHAT YOU NEED TO KNOW

1. Battle of Fredericksburg: In December 1862, 78,000 Southern troops defeated 122,000 Northerners at Fredericksburg, Virginia. General Lee defeated General Burnside.

2. Battle of Chancellorsville: In April and May 1863, 60,000 Southern troops defeated 133,000 Northern troops in Chancellorsville, Virginia. General Lee defeated General Hooker.

3. Battle of Gettysburg: In July 1863, 104,000 Northern troops defeated 75,000 Southern troops. General Meade defeated General Lee in the most consequential battle of the war. The Battle of Gettysburg is called the "high water mark of the South" because after this battle, the South receded.

4. Colonel Chamberlain's Bayonet Charge: Running out of ammunition, Union Colonel Chamberlain led a successful bayonet charge against the South at the Battle of Gettysburg.

5. Pickett's Charge: On the last day of the Battle of Gettysburg, General Pickett's 15,000 men suffered great casualties as they marched across a mile-long grass field to fight the Northern soldiers.

6. The Gettysburg Address: Abraham Lincoln's address honored the dead soldiers of Gettysburg and inspired Americans to fight so that a "government of the people, by the people, for the people, shall not perish from the earth."

7. General Grant in the West: General Grant had successes at Fort Henry, Fort Donelson, the Battle of Shiloh, and at Vicksburg. Lincoln named Grant the General-in-Chief of the Union Armies in 1863.

LOGIC
READING COMPREHENSION AND INFERENCE QUESTIONS

1. What can you infer from this lesson?

      a. Lee was a horrible general.

      b. Meade was a horrible general.

      c. Lee was an amazing general.

      d. Hooker was an amazing general.

Answer:

Which sentence(s) best supports this answer?

_____

_____

_____

_____

2. Place the following in chronological order, based on their leadership of the Northern Armies.

      a. Grant

      b. Meade

      c. Hooker

      d. Burnside

Answer:

3. Based on the lesson, you can infer that the Battle of Chancellorsville

      a. was a complete success for the South.

      b. was a complete loss for the North.

      c. was a waste of human life.

      d. was a Southern victory and loss.

Answer:

Which sentence(s) best supports your answer?

_____

_____

_____

4. Based on the Gettysburg Address, Abraham Lincoln

      a. was a believer in God.

      b. was an atheist.

      c. was a racist.

      d. believed that slavery was good.

Answer:

Which sentence(s) best supports this answer?

_____

_____

_____

5. Based on the lesson, Grant

      a. did what was needed to defeat the South.

      b. did not care about his soldiers.

      c. was a butcher.

      d. was indecisive.

Answer:

Which sentence(s) best supports this answer?

_____

_____

_____

RHETORIC
SHORT ANSWER QUESTIONS

Answer the following with a short essay (3-5 sentences):

1. How was General Grant different from Generals Meade, Hooker, and Burnside?

_____

_____

_____

_____

2. Based on this lesson, what is at least one battle strategy that Civil War generals used to win battles?

Answer:

_____

_____

_____

_____

_____

3. What made the Battle of Gettysburg more challenging for General Lee than the Battles of Fredericksburg and Chancellorsville?

Answer:

_____

_____

_____

_____

_____

_____

CASUALTIES OF THE CIVIL WAR

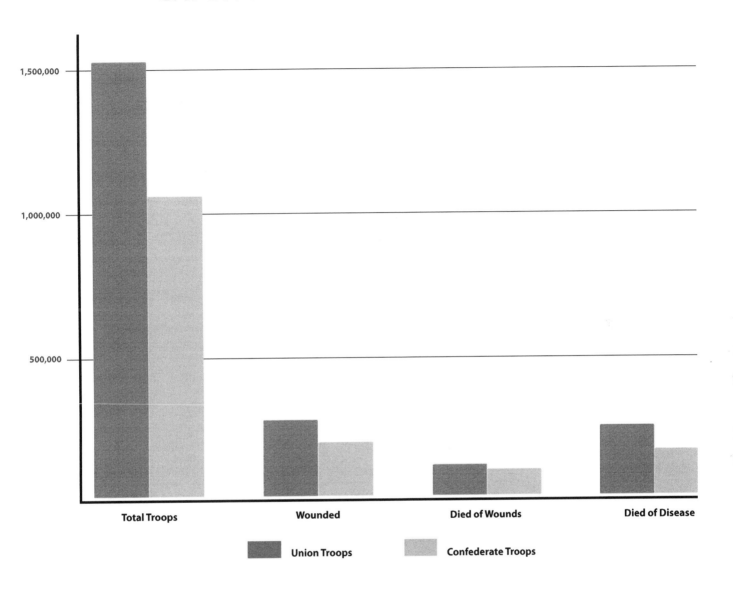

Total Troops   Wounded   Died of Wounds   Died of Disease

Union Troops   Confederate Troops

Answer these questions and test your knowledge.

1. Which side had greater casualties? _____

2. Which side had more troops in the war? _____

3. Which side defended their own states more than the other side? _____

4. What was the main cause of death for the Civil War soldier? _____

5. Did more than 1 million soldiers die in the Civil War? _____

CIVIL WAR BATTLES, 1861 - 1865

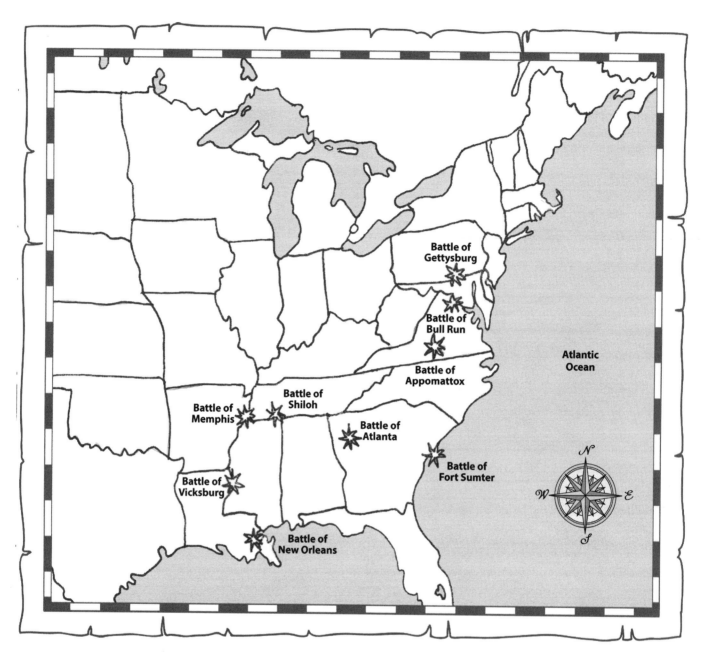

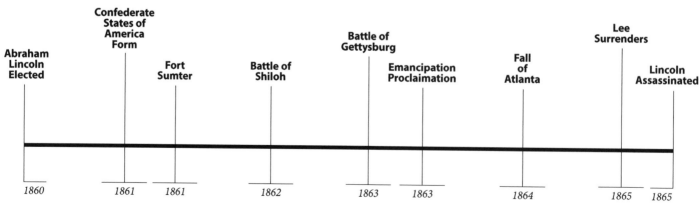

CHAPTER 64

UNCONDITIONAL SURRENDER GRANT AND LINCOLN'S REELECTION

General Grant

GRAMMAR
WHAT YOU NEED TO KNOW

1. **Civil War Casualties:** In the Civil War, over 620,000 were killed and 800,000 were wounded.

2. **Election of 1864:** In 1864, Republican Abraham Lincoln ran against Democrat General McClellan. McClellan wanted to end the war and let the Confederate States of America form. Lincoln and the Republicans wanted to defeat the South and end slavery in the South. Lincoln and the Republicans won the election.

3. **Copperheads:** Copperheads were Northern Democrats who promoted Confederate successes and sabotaged the U.S.A.

4. **Radical Republicans:** Radical Republicans wanted to end slavery in the entire country immediately.

5. **Conscription:** Conscription is when the government forces men to fight as soldiers. A synonym for conscription is the draft.

6. **General Phillip Sheridan:** Northern General Sheridan destroyed Southern forces in the Shenandoah Valley.

7. **General William Tecumseh Sherman:** Northern General Sherman led his soldiers on a "march to the sea," where his army burned a path 60 miles wide through Georgia.

LOGIC
READING COMPREHENSION AND INFERENCE QUESTIONS

1. Place the following in chronological order:

      a. Lincoln reelected

      b. Lincoln gives Gettysburg Address

      c. Battle of Gettysburg

      d. Grant named Union General-in-Chief

Answer:

2. Based on the lesson, you can infer that Grant

      a. did not attack enough

      b. moved too slowly

      c. moved too quickly

      d. attacked often and vigorously

Answer:

Which sentence(s) best supports your answer?

_____

_____

3. Based on the lesson, Grant's victories and Sherman's victories

      a. made the war last longer

      b. made the war less bloody

      c. helped Lincoln win reelection

      d. helped Lincoln lose reelection

Answer:

Which sentence(s) best supports your answer?

_____

_____

RHETORIC
SHORT ANSWER QUESTIONS

Answer the following with a short essay (3-5 sentences):

1. Why does the author write that Lincoln was the most reviled President in the history of the United States of America?

_____

_____

_____

_____

_____

_____

_____

2. How did the military successes of Grant, Sheridan, and Sherman help Abraham Lincoln get reelected?

Answer:

_____

_____

_____

_____

_____

3. Was General Sherman morally justified to lead his men on a "march to the sea," burning and destroying a path 60 miles wide through Georgia?

Answer:

_____

_____

_____

_____

_____

CIVIL WAR BATTLES, 1861 - 1865

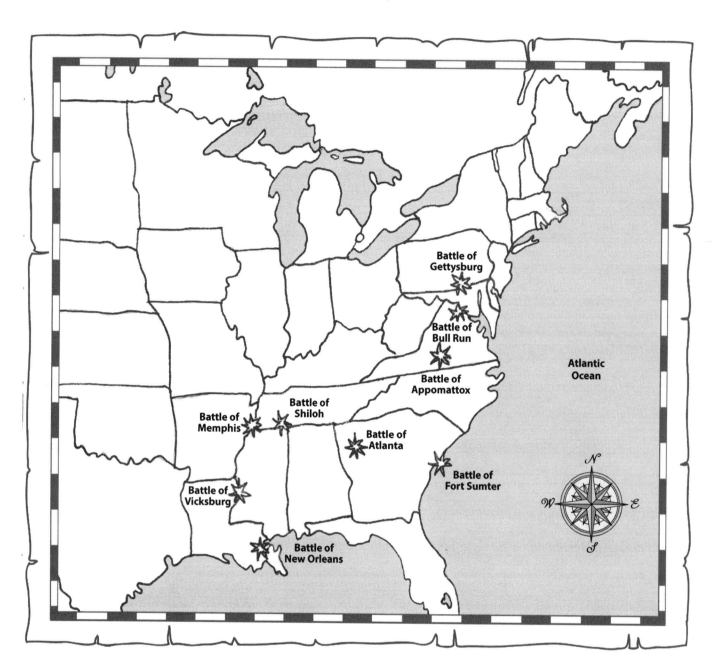

Answer these questions and test your knowledge.

1. On this map, which battle was most in the North? _____

2. Which battle was closest to the U.S. Capital? _____

3. Which three battles were on the Mississippi River? _____

_____

4. Which battle started the Civil War? _____

5. Which battle was the last battle of the Civil War? _____

Inflation in the South

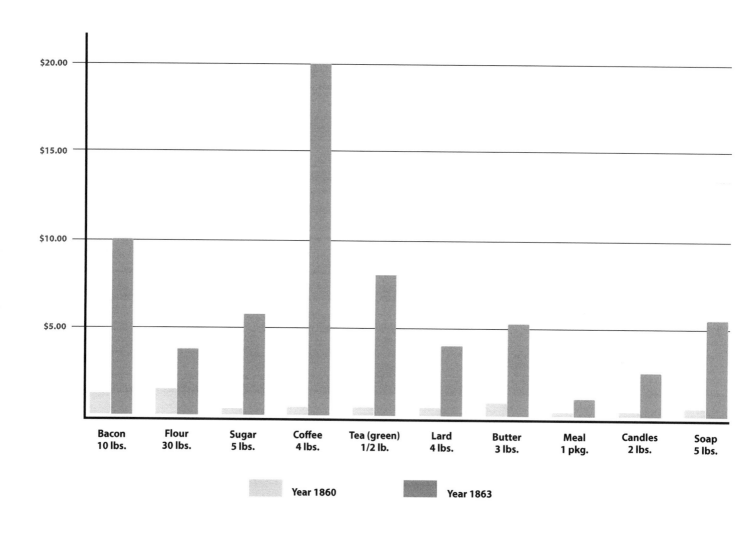

Bacon 10 lbs.	Flour 30 lbs.	Sugar 5 lbs.	Coffee 4 lbs.	Tea (green) 1/2 lb.	Lard 4 lbs.	Butter 3 lbs.	Meal 1 pkg.	Candles 2 lbs.	Soap 5 lbs.

Year 1860   Year 1863

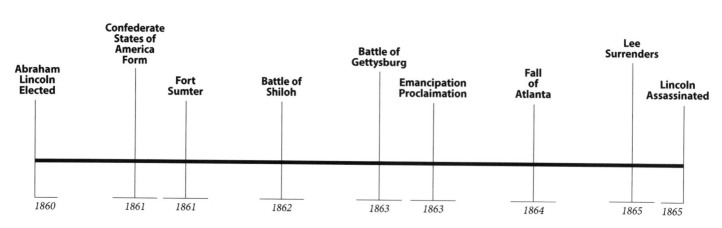

CHAPTER 65

THE END OF THE WAR AND LINCOLN'S ASSASSINATION

Lincoln is Assassinated

GRAMMAR
WHAT YOU NEED TO KNOW

1. **Army of Northern Virginia:** General Lee was the Commander of the Army of Northern Virginia. Lee's army was the main Southern army.

2. **Appomattox, Virginia:** At Appomattox, Virginia, General Lee surrendered to General Grant on April 9, 1865.

3. **Jefferson Davis and the End of the War:** After Lee surrendered, Davis called for all Southerners to resist and continue fighting. Davis was arrested and jailed.

4. **Lincoln assassinated:** Lincoln was assassinated in 1865 by Southern Democrat John Wilkes Booth.

5. **Radical Republicans:** Radical Republicans wanted to end slavery immediately after the war and they wanted to punish the Southern Democrats who had seceded from the Union.

LOGIC
READING COMPREHENSION AND INFERENCE QUESTIONS

1. Based on the lesson, you can infer that Lee's surrender

      a. didn't signal the end of the war for the South.

      b. was supported by C.S.A. President Jefferson Davis.

      c. was the real end of the Civil War.

      d. marked a complete success by Jefferson Davis.

Answer:

Which sentence(s) best supports this answer?

_____

_____

2. Based on the lesson, Grant's surrender terms to Lee can be described as

      a. harsh

      b. easy

      c. questionable

      d. amazing

Answer:

Which sentence(s) best supports this answer?

_____

_____

3. Based on his actions after Lee's surrender, what word best describes Jefferson Davis?

      a. convinced

      b. indecisive

      c. rebellious

      d. peaceful

Answer:

Which sentence(s) best supports this answer?

_____

_____

_____

4. Based on Lincoln's second inaugural address, what did Lincoln want to do to the Southerners who had seceded?

       a. punish them

       b. reward them

       c. forgive them

       d. ignore them

Answer:

Which sentence(s) best supports this answer?

_____

_____

5. Based on the lesson, Booth and his conspirators were most likely members of what political party?

       a. Democratic

       b. Republican

       c. Lincolnian

       d. Radical Republican

Answer:

Which sentence(s) best supports the answer?

_____

_____

RHETORIC
SHORT ANSWER QUESTIONS

Answer the following with a short essay (3-5 sentences):

1. Why did Booth assassinate Lincoln?

_____

_____

_____

_____

_____

_____

2. Describe Grant's surrender terms and what we can learn about Grant based on this.

Answer:

_____

_____

_____

_____

_____

INFLATION IN THE SOUTH

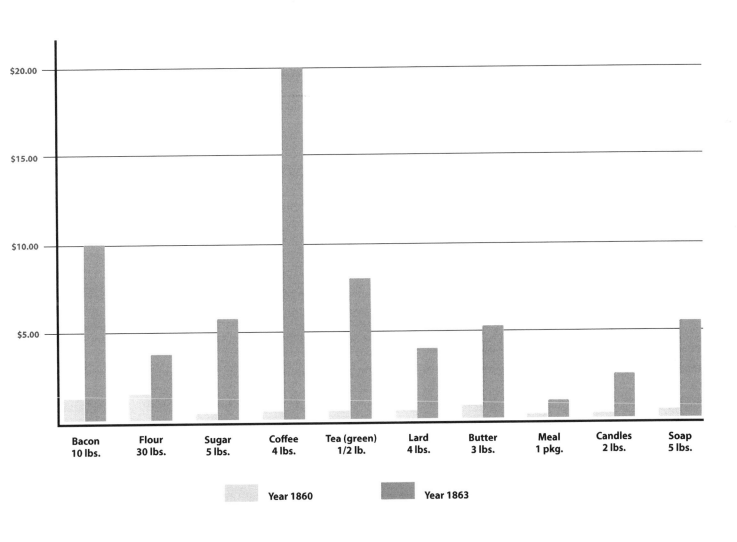

Year 1860	Year 1863

Answer these questions and test your knowledge.

1. During the war, did prices go up or down in the South? _____

2. About what was the cost of soap in 1863? _____

3. What was the cost of lard in 1863? _____

4. What product cost 40 times more in 1863 than it did in 1860? _____

5. Of the products listed, which saw its price increase the least in terms of percentage of its

   original price? _____

WAR DEATHS

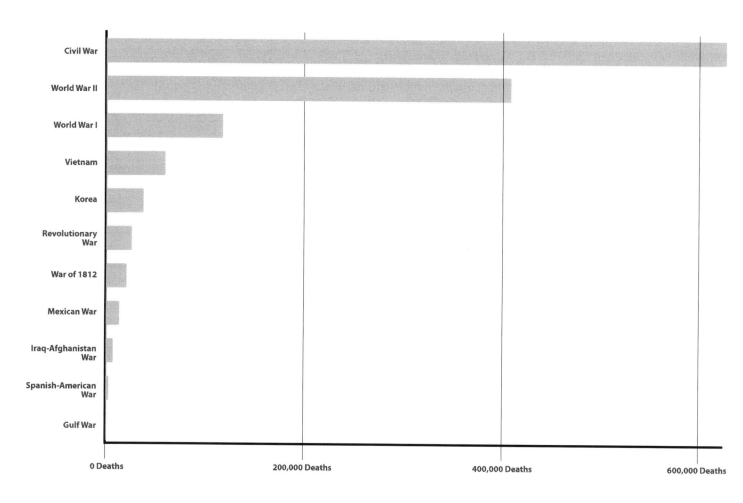

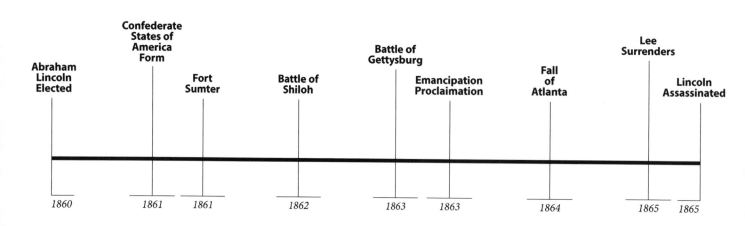

CHAPTER 66

WINNERS, LOSERS, AND LASTING CHANGES

Richmond, Virginia

Charleston, South Carolina

GRAMMAR
WHAT YOU NEED TO KNOW

1. 13th Amendment: The 13th Amendment ended slavery in the U.S.A. in 1865.

2. Lost Cause Myth: Writers have created a myth that Southerners fought for states' rights and would have ended slavery on their own. There is no evidence that any Southern state was considering ending slavery.

3. 14th Amendment: The 14th Amendment guarantees all born in the U.S.A. full citizenship rights. It was passed in 1868.

4. 15th Amendment: The 15th Amendment guarantees all citizens the right to vote. It was passed in 1871.

LOGIC
READING COMPREHENSION AND INFERENCE QUESTIONS

1. Based on the lesson, which statement is true?

  a. Left on their own, the evidence shows the C.S.A. would have ended slavery on their own.

  b. The C.S.A. made it illegal for any state to free their slaves.

  c. The North was unfair to force the Southerners to free their slaves.

  d. Lincoln and the Republicans wanted to keep slavery.

Answer:

Which sentence(s) best supports this answer?

_____

_____

_____

2. Based on the lesson, you can infer that the 13th, 14th, and 15th amendments

  a. were faithful to America's founding documents.

  b. went against America's founding documents.

  c. did not make any sense.

  d. were good for Northerners and bad for Southerners.

Answer:

Which sentence(s) best supports this answer?

_____

_____

3. Based on the lesson, the reasons for the Civil War

  a. stayed the same for the North from 1861 to 1865.

  b. changed for the North from 1861 to 1865.

  c. stayed the same for the entire country from 1861 to 1865.

  d. changed for the West from 1861 to 1865.

Answer:

Which sentence(s) best supports this answer?

_____

_____

_____

4. Based on the results of the Civil War, who or what lost the most?

     a. the slaves

     b. the North

     c. the South

     d. the West

Answer:

Which sentence(s) best supports this answer?

_____

_____

_____

5. Place the following in chronological order:

     a. 13th amendment

     b. Emancipation Proclamation

     c. Beginning of the Civil War

     d. 21st century

Answer:

RHETORIC
SHORT ANSWER QUESTIONS

Answer the following with a short essay (3-5 sentences):
1. How is the Declaration of Independence anti-slavery?

_____

_____

_____

_____

_____

_____

_____

2. In what ways is the Lost Cause Myth false?

Answer:

_____

_____

_____

_____

_____

_____

_____

3. What proof is there that the Civil War was fought over slavery?

Answer:

_____

_____

_____

_____

_____

_____

_____

_____

_____

WAR DEATHS

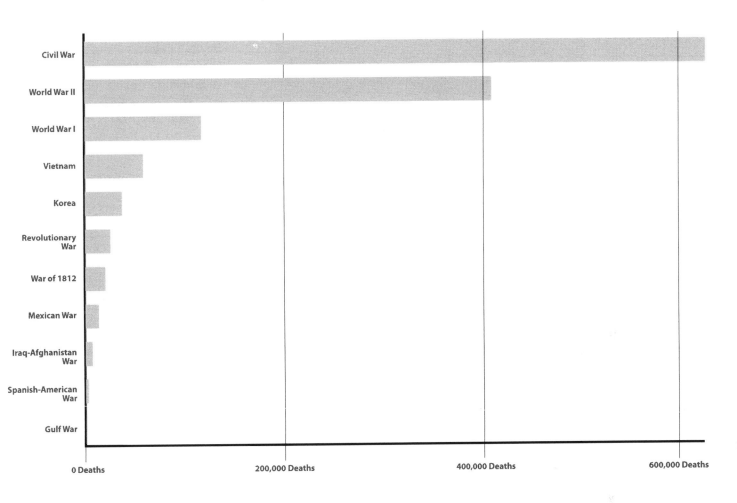

Answer these questions and test your knowledge.

1. Which U.S. war was costliest in terms of American lives? _____

2. On the graph, which war cost the least number of American deaths? _____

3. What has been America's second costliest war in terms of American lives? _____

4. Based on this graph, what has been America's least costliest war, in terms of American lives?

_____

5. Did more Americans die in the Revolutionary War or the Iraq-Afghanistan War?

_____

ACTIVITIES
UNIT 11

RHETORIC
OPEN-ENDED ESSAY

THE CIVIL WAR, COMPARE AND CONTRAST
BACKGROUND

Before the Civil War, the North and the South each hoped and believed its side would win in less than three months. Soldiers even signed up for only 90 days. However, the war lasted four long years, 1861–1865.

QUESTION

Compare and contrast the strengths and weaknesses of the North and the South before the war began. Decide which strengths and weaknesses were the most important for both sides. According to the evidence, was it inevitable for the North to win, or could the South have won?

THESE ARE TERMS YOU SHOULD BE FAMILIAR WITH TO ANSWER THE QUESTION:

Abraham Lincoln	Jefferson Davis	agriculture
railroads	U.S. Navy	immigration
slavery	Robert E. Lee	Ulysses S. Grant
Battle of Gettysburg	Jeb Stuart	Appomattox Courthouse

A. TAKING NOTES

Follow the structure below to write notes. Take notes on all terms.

ABRAHAM LINCOLN

What? _____

Who? _____

When? _____

Where? _____

Why? _____

Any other information? _____

_____

Was this person or term a strength or a weakness for the North or for the South? How?

_____

_____

_____

B. COMPARE AND CONTRAST

To **COMPARE** means to look at two or more objects and recognize what they have in common.

To **CONTRAST** means to look at two or more objects and recognize what they have different from each other.

For this assignment, fill in the chart below to analyze what the North and South had in common and in contrast.

NORTH CONTRASTS	COMMON	SOUTH CONTRASTS
industrial	speak English	agricultural
22 million	English political heritage	9 million
105,000 acres	part of North America	56,000 acres
free	similar laws	slave
many railroads	similar culture	few railroads
disliked slavery	the American Revolution	had slaves
strong federal government	Constitution	states' rights

C. DISCUSSION

When you share ideas with others, your ideas may be reinforced, rejected, or slightly changed. Listening to your classmates' ideas will help you form your own judgment. Likewise, if you are alone in a classroom or if you are learning with your teacher, it is important that you prepare all sides of an argument. Try to learn all sides of an argument and be prepared to defend all sides.

If you are in a classroom, each student should interview at least three classmates who do not sit next to one another. If you are in a classroom with one student, the one student should be able to discuss all possible answers to the question.

1. COMPARE AND CONTRAST THE STRENGTHS AND WEAKNESSES OF THE NORTH AND THE SOUTH BEFORE THE WAR BEGAN. DECIDE WHICH STRENGTHS AND WEAKNESSES WERE THE MOST IMPORTANT FOR BOTH SIDES. ACCORDING TO THE EVIDENCE, WAS IT INEVITABLE FOR THE NORTH TO WIN, OR COULD THE SOUTH HAVE WON?"

2. WHY DO YOU THINK THIS?/ WHAT IS YOUR EVIDENCE?

Student 1: _____

_____

Student 2: _____

_____

Student 3: _____

_____

REFLECTION

After you have written down all your classmates' responses, think about them and ask yourself the following questions. Write down your answers under your classmates' responses.

1. WHAT DO I THINK OF THESE CLASSMATES' ANSWERS? _____

_____

2. WHICH ARE THE THREE BEST ANSWERS? _____

_____

3. HAVE I CHANGED THE WAY I THINK? HOW? _____

_____

You should now have a chance to present your ideas in a class discussion. If somebody says something with which you disagree, speak up! In your discussion, you may find out he is actually right and you are wrong. All possible viewpoints should be stated and defended out loud. Test your ideas in class.